GOD ISN'T
IN A HURRY

GOD ISN'T IN A HURRY

Learning to Slow Down and Live

✦ WARREN W. WIERSBE ✦

Baker Books

A Division of Baker Book House Co
Grand Rapids, Michigan 49516

Published by Baker Books
a division of Baker Book House Company
P.O. Box 6287, Grand Rapids, MI 49516-6287

Printed in the United States of America

Library of Congress Cataloging-in-Publication Data

Wiersbe, Warren W.
    God isn't in a hurry : learning to slow down and live / Warren W.
Wiersbe.
      p. cm.
    ISBN 0-8010-9730-4
    1. Christian life—1960- 2. Rest—Religious aspects—Christianity. 3.
Patience—Religious aspects—Christianity. I. Title.
BV4501.2.W51835   1944
248.4—dc20   94-6529

For current information about all releases from
Baker Book House, visit our web site:
                http://www.bakerbooks.com/

CONTENTS

113871

1 GOD ISN'T
IN A HURRY

*A*lthough I was weary from a long flight, the sign on the mission guesthouse bulletin board made me laugh aloud. It said, "Lord, please make me patient— and do it right now."

Patience was one of the first lessons we had to learn in childhood. The child who does not learn to be patient is not likely to learn much of anything else. It takes patience to learn to read, to spell, to write, and to master multiplication tables. It even takes patience to grow! God has ordained that maturity is a slow process, not an instant experience; and I am glad that he arranged things that way. It gives me time to get accustomed to growing up.

Impatience is usually a mark of immaturity. At least James felt that way. "But let patience have its perfect work, that you may be perfect and complete, lacking nothing" (James 1:4). Little children think you have arrived at your destination when you stop for the first stoplight. A short wait in the doctor's office is unbearable. I once asked a lad in Scotland how many years he had left in school, and he replied, "I don't know, sir. I'm just trying to get through next week."

But adults have their share of impatience. Abraham got weary of waiting for the promised son; so he hurried and took Hagar as a second wife, and she bore him Ishmael.

Moses got impatient and killed a man. This necessitated forty years of postgraduate work in the pastures of Midian. Years later, Moses became impatient again, smote the rock, and lost a trip to the Holy Land.

"Do not be like the horse or as the mule," warns Psalm 32:9, and it is a warning that we need. The mule is stubborn and has a tendency to hold back. The horse is impulsive and wants to rush ahead. Personality differences may enter in here, but we all have the same problem—it is difficult to wait on God.

Part of the problem is that we are prone to walk by sight and not by faith. God assures us in his Word that he is busy on our behalf, but we still want to see something happen. At the exodus, the Israelites were sure that God had deserted them and destruction was on its way. Listen to that wind! See how dark it is! And yet God was working for his people in the wind and in the darkness. "All these things are against me," cried Jacob (Gen. 42:36) when, in reality, all things were working for him.

I believe that it was F. B. Meyer who used to say, "God's delays are not God's denials." They are usually the means which God uses to prepare us for something better. God is always at work for the good of his people, and he is working in all things (see Rom. 8:28). This includes the things that perplex us and that pain us. The only way God can teach us patience is to test us and try us, and the only way we can learn patience is to surrender and let God have his way.

God can grow a mushroom overnight, but he will take time to grow an oak or a giant sequoia. It took him thirteen years to get Joseph ready for the prime minister's office in Egypt, and he invested eighty years preparing

Moses for forty years of service. David was a youth when
Samuel anointed him king of Israel, but David had to experience a great deal of suffering before he finally ascended
that throne. We are the richer for it, because out of those
years of preparation came many of David's greatest
psalms.

Our Lord spent thirty years getting ready for three years
of public ministry. He patiently obeyed the Father's will
as he carried out that ministry. "My hour has not yet come,"
he told Mary (John 2:4). "Are there not twelve hours in the
day?" he asked his impatient disciples (11:9). God has his
times as well as his *purposes,* and to miss his times is to delay
his purposes.

When I was a student in seminary, I was privileged to
pastor a church on weekends. God blessed in many ways,
and at one point I was tempted to leave school and devote
my full time to the church. My faculty counselor set me
straight. "God has waited a long time for you to come
along," he reminded me, "and he can wait until you gradu-
ate. Don't sacrifice the permanent for the immediate." He
was right, and today I am glad I followed his counsel.

Perhaps the hardest place to be patient is in the furnace
of suffering. God does not always explain what he is doing
or why he is doing it. It is in the hour of suffering that we
need to "imitate those who through faith and patience
inherit the promises" (Heb. 6:12). "For you have need of
endurance, so that after you have done the will of God,
you may receive the promise" (10:36). Knowing that the
Father is near us and that he is working out his wonderful purposes ought to encourage us, but we often get impatient just the same.

"Why has God made me this way?" a suffering saint
once bitterly asked her pastor. Gently, he replied, "God has
not made you—*he is making you.*" How true! And how easy
it is for us to forget this truth!

If God can make a believer patient, then God can trust that believer with whatever is in his gracious will. But the school of patience never produces any graduates, and it never grants any honorary degrees. We are always learning, always maturing. Sometimes we fail the examination even before we know what the lesson is! No matter; our loving Father is guiding us and making us more like his beloved Son, and that is all that matters.

"Lord, make me patient!" God will answer that prayer, often in ways that will startle us. "And do it right now!" That prayer he cannot answer, for even almighty God must take time to turn clay into useful vessels. The best thing you and I can do is to stop looking at our watches and calendars and simply look by faith into the face of God and let him have his way—in his time.

2 THE HIGH COST OF SHORTCUTS

My wife and I were driving through the foothills of the Cumberland Mountains in Kentucky, and we decided to take a shortcut on a road that seemed inviting. What a road it turned out to be! It was used so infrequently that tortoises were on it, basking in the sun. (We picked one of them up and took it home to the children.) Any road that is safe for tortoises is the wrong road for people. The shortcut turned out to be uncomfortable, dangerous, and time-consuming.

I am sure that in many areas of life there are valid shortcuts that save both time and energy. Every cook has shortcuts that save time in the kitchen, and I suppose most skilled workers pass on their secret shortcuts to their apprentices. But in the areas of life that really count, such as building character and serving God, we need to beware of shortcuts.

For example, I have met people who are looking for shortcuts to understanding the Bible. They purchase study Bibles, filled with notes and encyclopedic facts, and yet they never seem to get a grasp of the truth of God's Word. Why? Because they are in a hurry and want to use a shortcut. They don't know the difference between facts and truths, between mental comprehension and spiritual apprehension. They pore over outlines and study charts and chase down cross-references, but they never take time to allow the Spirit of God to teach them.

Because there are no shortcuts in learning God's truth, there are no shortcuts in building godly Christian character. We study the Word of God that we might better know the God of the Word; and as we get to know him better, we become more like him. A reputation can be made—or lost—overnight, but it takes years to build character.

It comes as a shock to some Christians that God is more concerned about the worker than he is the work. Instead of preparing Joseph, God could have sent angels to provide for Jacob and his family, and he could have delivered Israel from Egypt by simply speaking the word. But he chose to take the long route and build leaders who would help him get the job done. We parents should follow the same approach with our own children. It is easier for you to mow the lawn or carry out the garbage than to motivate your children to do it, but they need to learn to obey and to work. The issue is not getting a job done; it is building character, and you never build character by taking shortcuts.

We cannot use shortcuts when it comes to understanding spiritual truth, building Christian character, or building the local church. The emphasis in the church today seems to be on methods and goals. There is nothing essentially sinful about either of these, provided they are not manmade shortcuts to achieve man-exalting goals. Some methods are unworthy of the gospel; in fact, they cheapen the gospel. Some goals are only the carnal projection of some leader's ego and have nothing to do with the work of God or the glory of God.

Jesus told a parable about two builders, one of whom was in a hurry and built his house without a solid foundation. Needless to say, the structure did not last. The other man took more time. He laid a foundation and built a house that withstood the storms. The shortcut approach was disastrous, not only to the house but also to the people in the house! This impatient builder learned the hard way the high cost of shortcuts.

Where there is life, there is growth; and the church ought to increase in both quality and quantity. But churches do not grow by addition; they grow by nutrition. True growth is from the inside out—at least the kind of growth that lasts. During more than forty years of ministry in many parts of the world, I have seen all sorts of schemes for building the church; and some of them, unfortunately, have worked— only to the detriment of the ministry. George Macdonald was right: "In whatever man does without God, he must either fail miserably, *or succeed more miserably.*"

If you are interested in the praise of men, then use the shortcuts and publicize your statistics. But if you are interested in the glory of God, stick with God's methods—the Word, prayer, witnessing, sacrifice, and suffering—and leave the results with him. After all, it is "God who gives the increase" (1 Cor. 3:7).

There are no shortcuts when it comes to solving life's problems. I don't mean the trivial problems that occasionally upset us. I mean those life-threatening problems that have long, deep roots and that produce bitter fruits. In my pastoral ministry, I have tried to counsel people with such problems. I have marveled at how long it took them to create the problem, and yet how quickly they expected the preacher and God to solve it!

I'm sure that medical doctors face the same situation. Many patients have hidden their symptoms for months, perhaps years, and then ask the doctor to give them a pill that will instantly cure them. I have conducted funerals for people who waited too long, and then it was too late.

Husbands and wives with marital problems, fathers and mothers with family problems, and individuals with deep personal problems all have a tendency to look for shortcuts; and the shortcuts only make the problem worse. "One of the great disadvantages of hurry," said Gilbert Chesterton, "is that it takes such a long time." A shortcut solution to a problem may alter the symptoms, but it can never deal with the causes. Like the false prophets in Jeremiah's day, these "quick counselors" heal people's hurts only slightly, "saying, 'Peace, peace!' when there is no peace" (Jer. 6:14).

Finally, there are no shortcuts when it comes to revival. The church desperately needs revival, but it is not going to come by quick and easy methods. Evan Roberts prayed for eleven years before the Welsh Revival broke out, and his ministry during that remarkable time broke him physically. More than one hundred thousand people were converted to Christ during that mighty awakening, but it was not the result of manufactured meetings (they were spontaneous) or manmade promotions. True revival goes deeper than that.

Some people have the idea that revival can be imported. After all, if something happened in Town A under the ministry of Brother B, then there is no reason why it cannot happen in Town C or D. Perhaps it will. Perhaps God in his sovereignty will deign to use a humble servant to bring the same spiritual awakening to others; but then again, perhaps he may not. We had better beware of using shortcuts, even consecrated shortcuts. "Without the Spirit of God, we can do nothing," said Charles Spurgeon. "We are as ships without wind, or chariots without steeds; like branches without sap, we are withered; like coals without fire, we are useless." True revival is not worked up; it is sent down. It is not imported from the outside; it must begin on the inside.

Exodus 13:17 suggests that God avoids shortcuts. When he delivered Israel from Egypt, "God did not lead them by way of the land of the Philistines, although that was near." God took the long route for the good of his people, and he usually takes the long route today.

Our "instant" society has so invaded the church that we are constantly looking for shortcuts. All of nature bears witness to the fact that God takes time to accomplish great works, and all of church history, including the Bible, vindicates this witness. It is true that God can, and occasionally does, bring about some great blessing in a short time, but the usual manner of his working is deliberate and at leisure.

I may be wrong, but I have the feeling that we are looking for shortcuts because we don't want to pay the price for doing things God's way. Travail in prayer, hard study, serious heart searching, and patient sowing of the seed have been replaced by methods that guarantee instant results. Results, yes; fruit, no. You cannot have fruit without roots, and you cannot have roots unless you dig deep; and that takes time.

I recently read again an address that Spurgeon gave to his Pastors' College students and alumni back in 1881, and I was struck by his closing words: "Do not be afraid of hard work for Christ; a terrible reckoning awaits those who have an easy time in the ministry, but a great reward is in reserve for those who endure all things for the elect's sake."

Beware of the high cost of shortcuts.

3   AN HOUR AT A TIME

*S*omebody once tried to frighten the cowboy entertainer Will Rogers by asking him, "If you knew you had only forty-eight hours to live, how would you spend them?"

The wise Rogers replied, "One at a time."

Some years ago a toy called Time-Wasters appeared on the market. Most people do not need much help when it comes to wasting time! Wasting time is a common sin, but you rarely hear anybody confess it. Instead, we hear the common complaint: "I just don't have time to do much anymore!" Yet the Lord graciously gives each of us the same amount of time. It is what we do with it that counts.

Let me make some suggestions that may help us make better use of our time and get more done for Christ.

Start your day with the Lord. I realize that different people have different schedules, but biblical examples and general experience seem to indicate that a morning devotional time is best. The Lord Jesus arose early in the morning to pray and commune with the Father (see Mark 1:35). The psalmist got up before dawn to meet God (see Ps. 119:147). Present your whole day to the Lord, every detail of your schedule, and give it to him to manage for you.

This will take the pressure off of you. It will also help you when things seem to fall apart because of interruptions or emergencies.

Plan your day. It is not only busy executives who need to plan their day, but also busy husbands, housewives, students, and senior citizens. Nobody can afford to waste time. I like to prepare the day's schedule the evening before, listing the jobs I have to do and the places I have to go. During the day, I refer to my list and have a good time checking off the work that has been completed. At the end of the day, I go over the list and make a new list for the next day. This simple plan has enabled me to accomplish far more than I could have accomplished without it.

Take "blessing breaks" during the day. Millions of people take coffee breaks two or three times a day, but very few take time for blessing breaks. What is a blessing break? It is a brief time of praise and prayer for the purpose of quieting the heart and getting new guidance and strength from the Lord. We especially need them when we feel nervous or frustrated or when we feel ourselves getting irritable. Just take a few minutes to focus on Christ, remember his love, quote a promise and, by faith, receive the grace needed for that hour. I have done this while in my car waiting for a train to pass, while in line at the supermarket, and even while standing in an elevator in a department store. Believe me, it helps!

Try to keep margins around your life. Practicing brinkmanship will only make you nervous and worried; and when you are in that condition, you cannot do your best. When your life lacks breathing space, then everything that happens is an emergency. Stay ahead on long-range projects. Use extra time to get ahead; you will save time in the long run.

When pastoring Moody Church, I had to prepare four messages each week plus a radio script, and the only way

I could do it was to work ahead. Then when there were interruptions and emergencies (nobody ever schedules a funeral), I was able to use my margins to good advantage.

Live to please God and fulfill his purposes for you. An old Roman proverb says, "When the pilot does not know what port he is heading for, no wind is the right wind." Paul said, "One thing I do" (Phil. 3:13). God does not expect you to do everything. He usually asks us to do what we enjoy the most and what we can do best. When duty becomes delight, you are always more efficient. Drudgery is opportunity with the heart taken out of it.

When you live to please God, you find it easier to say a gentle no to the well-meaning people who want to manipulate your life and an enthusiastic yes to the ones who have a God-ordained challenge for you. When you know God's will, you can make better decisions and stay off of time-wasting detours.

Learn to relax and enjoy leisure time. It is not a sin to take time off! Vance Havner warned us, "If we don't come apart and rest, we will come apart." One of my favorite preachers is William Sangster of London, who died in 1960 after three years of gradual paralysis. What a tornado of energy and ministry he was! Yet he himself confessed, "I rushed about too much. I talked too much. I was proud of my health and work. I never had time really to look. The trouble was in the will—I lashed the body on, imprisoned in a timetable." We are not sure, but Dr. Sangster might have lived longer if he had taken time to relax. Recreation ought to be just that—*re*-creation.

You and I do not number our hours. We number our days: "So teach us to number our days, that we may gain a heart of wisdom" (Ps. 90:12). "As your days, so shall your strength be" (Deut. 33:25). God can give us wisdom and strength for each day *if we let him*—wisdom to know what to do and strength to do it. The tragedy is that we are wasting today by worrying about tomorrow or regretting yesterday. And we will do the same thing tomorrow.

Wise Benjamin Franklin wrote: "Dost thou love Life? Then do not squander Time; for that's the stuff Life is made of." To put it another way, the person who kills time will soon discover that time is killing him. Time is God's gift to us, and it is a sin to waste it or merely spend it; we must *invest* it by doing his will.

"Are there not twelve hours in the day?" asked Jesus Christ (John 11:9), which suggests that he lived by a divine timetable, a good example for us to follow. There is always time for the will of God.

4 THE ECONOMY AND ETERNITY

The pressures and problems being created by the economy are affecting all of us. People who used to read only the comics or the sports page of the morning newspaper are now scanning the business section as well, hoping to find some glimmer of encouragement. Even missionary prayer letters testify that the problems are global.

An older generation, chastened by one depression, is afraid to be optimistic; and a younger generation, accustomed to security, is inexperienced at being pessimistic. Economic advisors are perplexed. In short, there is confusion, concern, and fear. We may soon be seeing the results of this situation in the increase in divorces, suicides, and admissions to mental hospitals.

I am not an economist, and I have no special counsel for the people who manage our money. But I do have a few suggestions for my Christian friends, young and old, as all of us seek to weather the storm.

The greatest danger that we face is that *we may forget we are Christians*. In our concern about prices, we may forget values. The "care of this world, and the deceitfulness of riches" may choke the Word in our hearts and rob us of a fruitful harvest of spiritual things.

We may forget that the first Christians were poor people, for the most part, whose leaders had to confess to beggars, "Silver and gold I do not have" (Acts 3:6). When Jesus reviewed the seven churches of Asia Minor, he told the wealthiest church it was poor and the poorest church it was rich.

I may be wrong, but I suspect that the economic situation is revealing problems as well as creating them. Some of our churches are embarrassed to discover that their priorities have been all wrong, and some of our families are learning that they have been spending their money for that which is not bread. Too many Christians have been caught up in what James Denney called "the multiplication of artificial necessities." Now we are paying for it.

But I am not suggesting that we all sell our goods, give the money to the poor, and then head for the caves and the simple life. Spiritual simplicity is a matter of priorities, not possessions. Abraham was a wealthy man, but he put the best that he had on the altar to glorify God. He did not, like Lot, have one eye on the world and the other on the heavenly city. His singleness of vision produced simplicity of life, even in the midst of affluence.

Yet do we really need all the things that other people have? Is life really measured by "the abundance of the things that we possess"? In today's throwaway society, can we still follow the old adage, "Make it do, or do without"? After all, there are Christian brothers and sisters in other parts of the world who have little or nothing while American believers suffer from overweight and other painful consequences of overeating.

My first suggestion is that we examine our priorities as individuals, families, and churches. Let's determine whether or not we are using our means to the glory of God.

At the same time, let's pray for those who are leaders in our churches and other evangelical ministries, that they will have wisdom to use God's money wisely. Even in times of great prosperity, nobody can afford to waste anything; and we need to be especially careful in times of economic difficulty.

My second suggestion is that we not panic. The church has weathered many a storm and, with God's help, it can weather this one. I am afraid that local church officers may become so overly concerned about budgets that they may stand in the way of progress. Nehemiah built the walls of Jerusalem "even in troublesome times" (Dan. 9:25). I have learned in my own pastoral ministry that the times are never right for a building program, an addition to the staff, or the expansion of the missionary budget. There is always a dark cloud on the horizon. "He who observes the wind will not sow, and he who regards the clouds will not reap" (Eccles. 11:4).

This is certainly not a time for inaction. When Jesus gave his commission to the early church, the times were not much different from what we face today. High taxes, military expenditures, low wages, and unemployment all combined to make a rather dismal picture. Yet the early Christians stepped out by faith, trusted God to meet their needs, sacrificed and served, and the gospel spread across the world.

Perhaps the key is found in that word *sacrifice*. I once heard the late Jacob Stam pray, "O Lord, the only thing most of us know about sacrifice is how to spell the word!" Our luxuries have become necessities, and we refuse to give them up for the sake of others. The day may come when some of us will have to give up a vacation in order to help keep a missionary on the field. We have forgotten that one of the purposes for laboring (apart from paying our own bills) is that we "may have to give him who has need" (Eph. 4:28).

I heard about a pastor who candidated at a church and was called, provided that he lived by faith. He asked the six men on the committee what they meant by living by faith. What it meant was that he have no stated salary but that he simply trust God for his needs. The candidate made a suggestion that cost him the church: "Each of you men has a salary, so why don't we put all of the salaries together, divide the total by seven and *all of us can live by faith.*"

Members of local church boards or finance committees have no right to ask a pastor or a missionary to make sacrifices that they themselves are not willing to make. We are all in this together. Our churches must continue to grow. We must send out missionaries. We must utilize the tremendous media resources we now have to share the gospel with the world. To retrench and retreat would not only deny the very faith that we preach, but also would give the enemy opportunity for further gains.

On the local level, we must focus on people. If we have a choice between brick and mortar or flesh and blood, let's invest in flesh and blood. When you make out your will, please don't give your church another stained-glass window or memorial pulpit. Help some student prepare for ministry. Provide for a pastoral intern who can assist your pastor and learn on the job. Set up a fund to assist retired missionaries.

A pastor friend shared with me the burden he has for his church, and his plans were solid and attainable. But his church board is so frightened by the economic situation that they refuse to launch out, even though funds are already available. Somebody needs to tell these men that a church never stands still: it moves forward or it slips backward. When board members start asking "Is it safe?" instead of "Is it God's will?" then the church is in trouble.

The ten spies at Kadesh-Barnea decided that entering the promised land was not safe, so they led the nation into forty years of wandering.

The church has always operated on the basis of faith. "Faith is not believing in spite of evidence; it is obeying in spite of consequence." That statement has often jolted me in my own ministry, but the jolts have been good for me. The heroes of faith named in Hebrews 11 were not low-risk people. Had they considered only the circumstances and left God out of the picture, they would never have made it into Hebrews 11!

Times of adversity are always times of opportunity. "For a great and effective door has opened to me," wrote Paul, "and there are many adversaries" (1 Cor. 16:9). When you look at the difficulties through God, they turn into opportunities, and you see open doors. But when you look at God through the difficulties, you slam the doors shut.

After all, we are not here to maintain religious organizations. We are here to win people to Christ and to build up his church. It was when Peter caught the fish that he found the needed money in its mouth! If we were catching more fish and building more churches, we would find God supplying the money. Unless we start more churches here at home, we may not be able to send more missionaries overseas. If ever there was a time when home missions and foreign missions needed to work together, it is now.

Are we willing to examine our priorities? Are we willing to stop wasting money on trivia? Are we prepared to make some sacrifices? Are we sincerely concerned about people?

Let each of us be fully persuaded in our own mind, and let no one judge another servant. Each of us must examine our own heart honestly; and "whatever He says to you, do it" (John 2:5).

5 DON'T FORGET TODAY

Whenever times are difficult, people tend to turn for relief in one of three directions. Some turn back to the good old days and escape into nostalgia. Others project themselves into the unknown future, either through the occult or the fantasy world of space exploration, science fiction, and video games. Still others turn within and lose themselves in themselves, either by mystical meditation or by drug-induced experiences.

But no matter which way people turn, they all have the same goal in mind: to escape the present. Unfortunately, we have a parallel situation in the church, and it is time we face it courageously and do something about it.

Let's begin with the Christian nostalgia trend. Nobody has a greater appreciation for the heritage of the church than I do. I have spent more than half of my life studying the history of preachers and preaching. I have taught the history of preaching to seminary students, and I have encouraged my pastor friends to get acquainted with the famous men and women of church history.

But I am not so fascinated by the past that I want to duplicate it today. Nor do I believe the past was necessarily better than the present. In fact, the people living in those days lamented that God was not doing for them what he had done in the days of their forebears!

One danger of this Christian nostalgia is that we fail to appreciate what God is doing in our day, the men and women he is blessing, and the progress that is being made. Another danger is our feeble attempts to duplicate the past, turning history into a formula for success. If we will but do what Moody and Finney and Spurgeon did, God will bless us as he blessed them. But Moody and Finney and Spurgeon did not always agree in what they did. Which formula are we going to use?

Solomon gives us a timely warning in Ecclesiastes 7:10: "Do not say, 'Why is it that the former days were better than these?' For it is not from wisdom that you ask about this" (NASB). You don't move ahead by constantly looking in a rearview mirror. The past is valuable as a rudder to guide us but not as an anchor to drag us back. We must learn from the past, but we must not live in the past.

If my research is correct, the great men of the past, such as Moody and Spurgeon, were successful because they had their spiritual roots in the Word, they let God do what he wanted to do at that time, and they were not afraid of something new. Moody was a generation ahead of his time. He was on the cutting edge of the church, moving into new territory with new approaches that, to us today, are old hat.

Let me add a word of warning to my pastor friends: don't try to imitate the great preachers of the past. The Word of God never changes; it is always relevant to the human heart. But it needs to break forth in freshness and vitality in each generation.

One preacher imitates the old Puritan divines and bores his congregation with fifty messages from Nahum. Another preacher adopts the folksy approach of a Moody or the vivid oratory of a Talmadge. But why not just be yourself? God wants you, like John the Baptist, to be a voice and not an echo, a burning light and not a weak reflection.

The escape into the future is quite another matter. Does this happen to Christians in the church? Of course it does! Have you ever attended a prophecy conference where the emphasis was totally on what God will do in the future, not on what he wants to do through his church now? Have you ever met a sincere believer who can draw charts of future events and explain the most obscure biblical prophecy, and yet who has no love for God's people or concern for the lost?

I have studied Bible prophecy and preached at prophetic conferences. I know that a large portion of the Bible is devoted to prophecy. But I have also noted that the biblical prophets usually related their message to the present. They did not explain future events in order to entertain the curious or give false hope to the disobedient. The prophetic Scriptures tell us what God will do in the future so that his people know how to act in the present. They were given not for escape, but for enlightenment.

The prophet Amos preached to a generation of people who said that they yearned for "the day of the LORD" (Amos 5:18). They were wrapped up in the greatness of Israel's future, and yet were living selfishly at a time when sacrifice and service were desperately needed. Amos cried out: "Woe to you who desire the day of the LORD! For what good is the day of the LORD to you? It will be darkness, and not light" (v. 18). We preach, teach, and sing about the coming of the Lord as though seeing Jesus Christ will be all reward and no reckoning or responsibility. People with that attitude need to ponder our Lord's parable about the careless servant (Luke 12:41–48).

Again, a word to my preacher friends: By all means, preach the great prophetic Scriptures, but be sure you tie them to life and ministry today. The return of Jesus Christ is a great motivating force in the church, encouraging us to keep our lives clean, to serve others, and to use our opportunities to the fullest. We are certain of the future; therefore, let's be busy in the present. The best way to prepare for meeting Christ at any time is to do his will right now. Those who use prophecy as an escape from present responsibility will one day have a rude awakening.

Now, for the third group—those who turn within and try to escape reality with mystical experiences of one kind or another. The popularity of such things as yoga, transcendental meditation, the imported Oriental cults, and drugs is evidence that many people are retreating into themselves in order to become isolated and insulated from reality. We pity them, and yet perhaps we are indulging in similar "Christian" practices in our churches.

I fear that this emphasis on escape has crept into some of the so-called deeper life teaching in our day. Again, I have shared in many conferences where the emphasis has been on a deeper experience with the Lord. I have scores of books in my library written by the masters of the inner spiritual life, and I have read them carefully. The true biblical deeper-life message will not permit the believer to escape. We fellowship with God in a deeper way that we might go to the world and be better servants. God is our refuge that he might be our strength, so that we might go back into the battle and win some victories (see Ps. 46:1).

Too many Christians today are looking for a deeper experience for the sole purpose of enjoying it themselves. The lost world can tumble into hell around them, but it makes no difference. They are enjoying the Mount of Transfiguration and, like Peter, they want to stay there and bask in the glory. Instead of being channels of living water, they are Dead Seas, religious swamps with stagnant waters that kill.

There is a proper Christian mysticism, a personal fellowship with God that includes hearing his voice in the Word, meditating on his greatness, and sharing his love. Such worship—both personal and as a church body—is absolutely essential to Christian growth and guidance. "Abide in Me!" was our Lord's command (John 15:4), and we must obey it.

But the same Book that tells me to go "through the veil" also commands me to go "outside the camp, bearing His reproach" (Heb. 10:19; 13:13). Our rest in the green pastures is preparation for our walk through the dark valley. We receive that we might give; we enjoy his love that we might share it with others. Any deeper-life experience that isolates us from a world in need is counterfeit and dangerous.

I suppose the one thing we need more than any other is balance. We dare not cut ourselves off from the past, yet we must not live in the past. We need the encouragement of biblical prophecy, but it must be practical. We must have times of deeper fellowship with Christ, but they must equip us for wider service. Whether we look back, ahead, or within, the test is always the same: Will this truth make me a better Christian servant today?

Let's not neglect today. It is today that God is speaking and working. It is today that we have opportunities to love and serve people in the name of Christ. If we are going to make a success of today, we will need the enrichment of the past, the enlightenment of the future, and the encouragement of our present communion with the Lord.

Blessed are the balanced!

6 No Time for Second Opinions

A farmer with a severe leg rash visited a specialist and endured a series of tests. The doctor told him, "You will have to get rid of your dog. You're allergic to him." As the patient was leaving, the doctor asked, "Are you going to sell your dog or give him away?"

"Neither one," said the patient. "I'm going to get me one of those second opinions I've been reading about. It's easier to find another doctor than a good bird dog!"

We chuckle at this true story, but our farmer friend illustrates a sad characteristic of human nature: we are prone to look for the easy way out—another opinion—rather than face facts and do what ought to be done. We are like the trucker who didn't like the strange sound in the motor, so he loosened a fender and manufactured a noise to drown it out.

No doubt it is wise to get a second opinion in matters medical, but it can be unwise to get a second opinion in matters spiritual. Once God has spoken on a subject, the matter is settled. We can consult no higher source of wisdom, we can appeal to no higher court. "Thus saith the Lord!" is as wise and as high as we can get.

This desire for a second opinion was the beginning of Baalam's downfall. (If you have forgotten the account, you will find it in Numbers 22–24.) God clearly told Baalam what he was to do and say, and at first he obeyed God's command. But Balak the king knew how to influence the double-minded prophet. Balak kept suggesting that Baalam look at the situation from a different viewpoint. Each time Baalam blessed the Israelites, Balak moved him to a different location, hoping for different results.

It was Eve's interest in a second opinion that led Adam into sin and, as a result, plunged humanity into sin, death, and condemnation. "You have only heard one side of the story," said Satan, "and what you have heard may not be true. What God has not told you is that this tree can make you wise, and even make you like God." Our first parents fell for the second opinion—and fell.

It was Mark Twain who said, "It's not what I don't understand about the Bible that bothers me. It's what I do understand." When once we understand the will of God, revealed in the Word of God, we need no second opinion. Our responsibility is simply to accept what God says, be thankful for it, and obey it willingly. If we reconsider duty and look for a second opinion, we are putting ourselves into a dangerous position. Satan delights in tempting the saint who hesitates on the path of duty. The adversary makes sure that there is a bypath available, one that parallels the true road just long enough to give the pilgrim a false assurance that he is, after all, doing the will of God.

Those of us who minister the Word often meet undecided Christians who run from preacher to preacher in search of the will of God. We have learned a long time ago that these "gospel gadflies" are not looking for the will of God—they are looking for a second opinion, hoping to meet a pastor or a Bible teacher who will tell them what they want to hear. They have already decided what they are going to do, but they want a spiritual leader to endorse and bless them.

One of the saddest stories in Scripture is that of the disobedient prophet (1 Kings 13). God instructed the man to deliver his message to wicked King Jeroboam, and then to get away as soon as possible. He was not even to eat with anyone. Unfortunately, the prophet sat down under an oak, and the tempter (using the lips of an old backslidden prophet) caught up with him and led him into sin. The young prophet's disobedience cost him his life. When this prophet reconsidered the will of God and looked for a second opinion, he forsook the path of blessing and forfeited his life.

The desire for a second opinion about the will of God indicates that we are proud. Instead of bowing before his will, we examine it and evaluate it. We come to the conclusion that God is making a mistake. Or, we conclude that we have made a mistake and need to examine the matter from a different viewpoint. This makes us the judge of God's will, and he never called us to judge his will. He called us to do his will.

Let me make it clear that I am not suggesting that perplexed Christians ought never to seek prayerful spiritual guidance from mature saints. All of us have learned to appreciate the wise counsel of godly friends. What I am suggesting is that we watch our motives very carefully. Am I consulting with my friend because I sincerely want guidance, or because I am hoping he or she will find a loophole through which I can escape? Going back to our allergic farmer: am I looking for someone who will tell me to keep the bird dog?

When Jesus told the rich young ruler to sell all he had and join Jesus' disciples, the man went away in great sorrow. The Bible does not tell us where he went, but I wonder if he didn't seek out some doctor of the law and get a second opinion to salve his conscience. The Jewish Sanhedrin listened to the message of the apostles and carefully examined the miracle performed on the lame man, but they rejected the truth. They went to scholarly Gamaliel for a second opinion, and Gamaliel gave them the worst possible counsel: "Wait and see." While they were waiting, salvation passed them by.

General Omar Bradley said, "In war there is no second prize for the runner-up." We may paraphrase that statement: "In the Christian life there is no second prize for the one who has second thoughts about the will of God." What we may call spiritual reconsideration is usually an excuse for not doing our duty. We are looking things over from a different viewpoint, searching for that second opinion that will permit us to have our own way. Well, God may allow us to have our own way, and to pay for it. "And [God] gave them their request, but sent leanness into their soul" (Ps. 106:15). They got what they wanted but wished they hadn't!

When David was in the cave, he longed for a drink of water from the well in Bethlehem. He didn't issue a command; he simply breathed the longing to himself. But two of his soldiers were so close to their king and so attentive to his desires that they broke through the enemy lines, dipped out the water, and brought it to David. Oh, that we Christians had such a relationship to our King of kings! Oh, that his least desire were a burning commandment in our hearts!

When our heart's desire is to please our Lord because we love him, there will be no time for second thoughts or second opinions. Instead, we will echo the words of the Savior: "I delight to do Your will, O my God, and Your law is within my heart" (Ps. 40:8).

Which will it be—first-love obedience, or second-opinion disobedience?

7 CONTEMPORARY OR TEMPORARY?

*A*certain word has become important in our evangelical vocabulary in recent years. It is the word *contemporary*. I hear about "contemporary music," "contemporary preaching," and "contemporary worship services." Some of us who have been around for a few years are starting to feel intimidated, wondering if we are still contemporary!

It is my understanding that the word *contemporary* simply means "existing, living, or occurring at the same time." In my library, I have a *Dictionary of Contemporaries*. The book lists the names of famous people who lived and worked in the same historical periods.

However, in recent years, the word *contemporary* seems to have taken on an additional meaning—"not traditional, recent as opposed to ancient." It is this definition that disturbs me.

Take the matter of so-called contemporary music. *Contemporary to whom?* Most families have at least three generations living, and some have four. Is the music contemporary to me, my son, or my uncle? After all, we are all living at the same time! It is my guess (and I am not a musicologist) that contemporary music probably means "contemporary to whatever kind of music is popular in the secular world at that time." Of course, I could go on and discuss the question *"Which* world of secular music?" but I think you get the idea.

Consider, if you will, the so-called contemporary worship service. I participated in such a service one Sunday evening, and I came away less than satisfied, although I hold in high esteem the other people who participated in it. What made the service contemporary? In place of a pulpit we had a music stand. We added a guitar to the organ and the piano. Instead of hymnals we followed words flashed on a screen from an overhead projector. The song leader did not stand to direct the singing; instead, he sat on a barstool and led us, between chatty little pep talks. It was casual and informal. For the life of me, I could not figure out what made it contemporary. *Contemporary to what?*

When I used to preach at street meetings, we used guitars and sometimes a small portable organ, but we did not talk about being contemporary. It was just too difficult to carry the piano and the organ all over northern Indiana! I see no reason why a local church cannot change its services and do something different, but why call it contemporary? If a preacher wants to dramatize his sermon, or even preach in dialogue with another minister, nothing in the Bible prohibits it. But why call such preaching contemporary? *Contemporary to what?*

I think we have confused novelty and change and have hidden this confusion under the guise of being contemporary. Change for the sake of change is simply novelty, and it does not last. Change for the sake of improvement is progress, and progress is what we need. The sad thing about the contemporary emphasis is that it may keep us from diagnosing the real sickness in the church and securing the remedy. We are rearranging the furniture while the walls are falling down.

The church must always minister to present generations. In order to do this well, it must understand what people are thinking, what they are seeking, and what authority they are respecting. But this does not mean we must become like the secular world in order to get a hearing. Identification with the world and its needs is one thing; imitation of the world and its foolishness is quite another. The Pharisees repelled sinners by their sanctimonious piety, while Jesus attracted sinners by his compassion and concern. Campbell Morgan said that the church did the most for the world when the church was the least like the world, and he was right.

Most honest believers will admit that some contemporary music carries a message and is not offensive. (After all, the songs we enjoy—the good old hymns of the faith—were once new and contemporary and criticized!) We do not want to get into the habit of rejecting everything that is new and praising everything that is old. But neither do we want to fall into the trap of mistaking novelty for progress and cheap imitation for creative change. No ministry can afford to become a museum that enshrines the past, but neither can it afford to become a chameleon that spends all its time adjusting to the present.

The roots of our ministry go deep into the past, whether we like it or not: the creation, the call of Abraham, the giving of the law, the death and resurrection of Christ, the coming of the Spirit. But the fruits of our ministry must be in the present to meet the needs of people today. In that fruit is the seed for more fruit, which guarantees our ministry in the future. Biblical ministry is both timely and timeless. We are stewards who bring out of our treasury "things new and old" (Matt. 13:52).

I suggest that we drop the word *contemporary* unless we are going to use it in its correct meaning. The abuse of the word has only created problems. I also suggest that we learn to distinguish between true progress and cheap novelty. I, for one, am tired of hearing immature Christian entertainers ridicule our spiritual heritage in the name of contemporary evangelism. Finally, I suggest that if the younger generation expects the older generation to appreciate their expressions of worship, they might try learning to appreciate the heritage that we senior saints hold dear.

The danger, of course, is this: What people think is contemporary may turn out to be simply—*temporary*.

8 "QUIET TIME"— QUITE A TIME!

I suppose that, over the years, more people have asked me about the believer's quiet time (or devotional life) than about any other discipline of the Christian life. Most of us understand what is involved in witnessing, church membership, giving, and serving, but when it comes to this nebulous thing called the quiet time, many people find themselves baffled.

That was my situation when as a teenager I trusted Christ many years ago. I knew that I was supposed to read my Bible daily and spend time in worship and prayer, but I wasn't quite sure how to do it. Fortunately for me, some mature Christians gently instructed me. During my first year at seminary, I had a fine roommate who was disciplined in his devotional life; he encouraged me by his good example.

Let's begin with the obvious question: Why have a devotional life? Why take time every single day to read the Word, worship God, and pray? Let's get one thing clear from the start: We don't do it only because it is an obligation, but because it is an opportunity. Once you make your daily quiet time only an obligation, you have robbed it of being a blessing and have turned it into a potential burden. More Christians go on guilt trips over their undisciplined prayer life than perhaps any other personal problem.

Spending time daily with Christ in the Word and prayer should be an experience to enjoy and not an event to endure. Imagine a newly engaged fellow saying with a groan, "Well, I have a date this evening, and I have to spend three hours with Lucy!" Or picture a child lamenting the fact that Grandma and Grandpa are coming for a visit!

Two words have rescued me from devotional doldrums: *reality* and *relationship*. The material world around us appears to be the real world, but it is not. "The world is passing away," John wrote (1 John 2:17); Paul reminded the Corinthians that "the things which are seen are temporary, but the things which are not seen are eternal" (2 Cor. 4:18). A. W. Tozer used to remind us that the Bible world is the real world. When you spend time alone with the Lord, you are in contact with reality, the things that matter most, the things that will last.

But you are also building a relationship, and in building that relationship, you are building your own character and ministry. Jesus warned us, "Without Me, you can do nothing" (John 15:5). If we abide in Christ, then we can bear fruit for his glory. Your relationship with Jesus Christ is the most important single relationship in your life. Everything else flows out from it.

If you will just keep in mind what your devotional life means to him, it will encourage you. He longs for our fellowship; he wants to share his life with us. If Jesus Christ were living in a house up the street from you, and if his door were always open, you would rush up the street to visit him. But he is even closer to you than that.

Of course, your daily devotional time also means something to you personally. You need it; we all do. I dread to think of what our daily life would be like if we failed to start the day at the throne of grace. Life is sometimes difficult enough even when we do cultivate a satisfying quiet time. What would it be like if we ignored him completely?

We may not realize it, but our daily devotional life also means something to others. We certainly ought to be easier to get along with if we have spent time alone with the Master. The family that prays together, stays together, but it is also helpful if the members of the family learn how to pray alone. Corporate worship is only as good as what each person brings to it, and that means each of us must spend time alone with the Lord.

When the Old Testament priest burned the incense at the altar—a picture of prayer, according to Psalm 141:2—you can be sure that his friends and family knew about it, for he carried with him the fragrance of that experience. If you and I are taking time daily to meet the Lord, others will know it, for our lives will show it.

How, then, do we go about setting up a satisfying devotional life? We know that this daily experience is important to the Lord, to us, and to others. But what steps do we take to make it work? Again, two words have helped me: *habit* and *system*.

In our free society, the word *habit* is not often heard; if it is, some Christian is sure to sneer, "Legalism!" I thank God for good habits. They save me time and energy all day long. You and I are in the habit of bathing, eating, brushing our teeth, and perhaps doing a dozen other things, and yet nobody accuses us of being legalists who are caught in a trap. There are many decisions in the course of a day that are made for us by habit. We don't argue; we act.

Once you get into the habit of spending time daily with the Lord, you have won 90 percent of the battle. I don't know what the best time of day is for you. I like to start my day with the Lord, but shift-workers may prefer a different schedule. Mothers who must get their children off to school early in the morning may find that their quiet time goes better after the uproar has ceased. You and the Lord must work out the schedule. One of the *worst* things you can do is try to imitate some great saint who arose at four each morning and spent three hours in prayer. That may not be your style.

Along with habit, you need *system.* People who open the Bible any place and read what they open to are turning the Word of God into a book of magic. Would you read any other book that way? And those people who have favorite passages and read them over and over are making as great a mistake; both groups are robbing themselves of the whole Word of God. All Scripture is inspired; all Scripture is profitable; and people are supposed to live by *every* word of God (see Matt. 4:4).

Once again, you and the Lord must work out the system that is best for you, but I will make some suggestions. I like to read through the Bible regularly, and I begin in Genesis 1, Psalm 1, and Matthew 1, and keep reading. I may not read three complete chapters a day, because sometimes the Spirit stops me on one verse or paragraph, but that is still my pattern. This approach gives me a good balance of different portions of Scripture, so that I don't feel bogged down in any one place.

There are a number of fine Bible reading calendars available, so ask your pastor or local Christian bookseller to recommend one. The calendar worked out many years ago by Robert Murray M'Cheyne is still one of the best. He prepared it in 1842 for his congregation in Dundee, Scotland, and it has been used ever since by believers around the world. The late D. Martyn Lloyd-Jones used to enthusiastically recommend it. I believe it is published today under the title *Daily Bread.*

We need system not only in our Bible reading but also in our praying. Many churches publish weekly prayer lists, as well as missionary prayer lists, that enable the members to intercede systematically for one another. I use several lists published by various mission boards (no need to be "listless" in our praying). As far as personal requests are concerned, I have divided them into seven lists, one for each day of the week, plus a list that I use every day. From time to time, I review and revise these lists. What a delight it is to mark "Answered!" beside the requests that the Lord has granted.

Again, you must not copy me or Robert Murray M'Cheyne or any other Christian; but whatever you do, be systematic about it. Using prayer lists does not mean you are grieving the Spirit or preventing him from impressing you with a special burden. But the use of lists means that your praying becomes precise and specific (instead of "Lord, bless the missionaries") and you can keep a record of your spiritual transactions at the throne of grace. The fact that some of the greatest Christians I have ever met have used such a system is proof enough to me that the system must work. The older I get, the more my memory tricks me; I find that I must write down prayer requests or else they will be forgotten.

To be sure, there are dangers that we must avoid as we develop a satisfying devotional life. The first one, of course, is the danger of system and habit becoming routine. The devotional time can seem to be alive and yet be dead. How easy it is to read the assigned chapters and pray through the daily requests and still derive little or nothing from the experience. Habit without heart rapidly becomes routine. However, this danger is present in *any* meaningful experience of life, including marriage, and must not prevent us from persevering in our spiritual exercises.

One way to keep your devotional time from degenerating into a mere routine is to make sure you keep it on a relationship basis. You are not reading a Book or praying about needs; you are fellowshiping with the Son of God through the Word and prayer. Keep it personal and intimate and you will be less likely to lose the fervor and leave your first love. Always be open and honest with God. Never pray anything that you really do not mean. Honestly confess to the Lord that you are weary, that you have a headache and are having a difficult time meditating on the Word. He knows and understands.

If your favorite translation of the Bible has become so familiar to you that it no longer communicates God's truth forcefully, ask your pastor to recommend another translation for your devotional reading. Over the years I have read through my King James Version many times, as well as several dependable modern translations; it has been an enriching experience.

However, beware of turning your devotional time into a spiritual olympics! There is no special merit in reading a certain number of chapters or verses each day or in praying through a certain number of prayer requests. (A woman in a church I pastored used to ask me to remember "twenty-seven unspoken requests," but I was never quite sure how to do it.) We must take time to be holy, and this means chewing on the Word of God and not gulping it down as though we were at a religious fast-food restaurant. When two people who love each other are spending time together, they don't look at the clock or count the number of words they use in their conversation.

What about the use of a devotional book? Never use it as a substitute for your Bible! Read it after you have read God's Word and let the Spirit give you food from Scripture.

Perhaps the most important thing is that we carry into the day the enrichment received in our devotional time. I have often had the experience in the morning of reading in my Bible just the words that I needed later that day. How many times God has given guidance, confirmed decisions, issued warnings, and granted promises just when I needed them most. Your Father knows what you need and, if you permit him, he will speak to you day after day through his Word, and tell you how he plans to meet those needs.

Beside routine and trying to set records, there is the danger of turning your devotional time into a Bible-study time. Every believer needs to spend time seriously studying the Word of God, using the best helps available, but the quiet time is not the time for commentaries, concordances, and comparing translations. (To be sure, there is nothing wrong with investigating anything you read that puzzles you, but that is not the main purpose of the quiet time.)

I spend many hours a week in Bible study, but during my quiet time, I simply read the Word and receive it as though my Father were speaking to me personally. I ask the Spirit to lead me into the truth he wants me to receive that day. If I do see a passage that can be developed into a message, I note it, but I don't spend the rest of the time preparing a sermon. Even a good thing like a new sermon outline could become a detour that might affect my personal relationship with the Lord. (Preachers, take note!)

As you get involved in a systematic and regular devotional time, you will learn by experience just what the Lord wants you to do. If you encounter some problems, consult with some of the mature believers in your church or chat with your pastor about it. There are really no new spiritual problems, so somebody is bound to have the answer.

If you find yourself getting careless and neglecting your quiet time, confess it to the Lord and start over again. The victorious Christian life, said Alexander Whyte, is a series of new beginnings. Over the weeks and months, your heart will be enlarged and your life so enriched that neglect of your prayer time will become a rare thing.

David's heart thirsted for God as a panting deer thirsted for water in the desert. Jacob would not let the Lord go until he had blessed him. Moses prayed to be privileged to see the glory of God. Even our Lord Jesus Christ rose up early in the morning that he might spend time with the Father in prayer. If the perfect Son of God needed to meet the Father each day, how much more do we need to meet him!

The devotional time is a wonderful opportunity for us to please the Lord, grow in Christian character, and be of greater help to those who need us. When, like Mary of Bethany, we spend time at the feet of Jesus, we are choosing that good part which can never be taken from us.

9 KEEP THE WORD IN YOUR MOUTH

I ran across a quotation that started me thinking, and I want to share my thoughts with you. The quotation is from the Puritan preacher and writer Thomas Manton (1620–1677). He said, "What is the reason there is so much preaching and so little practice? For want of meditation."

Now, no honest Christian will deny that we have today a great deal of preaching. In local churches, over radio and television, in conferences, in home Bible-study groups, and in many other ways, God's Word is being shared. But I believe that this same honest Christian will have to admit that there is today a breakdown between the hearing of the Word and the practicing of it in daily life. People mark their Bibles, fill their notebooks, and file away their precious cassettes; but somehow the power of the Word never gets into the decisions and activities of daily life.

Manton may have hit upon the cause: we do not take time to meditate on what we have learned. The truth gets into our notebooks (and possibly into our heads), but it never gets to the heart. What digestion is to the body, meditation is to the soul. If you ate nourishing food but never digested it, you would slowly die.

I wonder if some of our Bible-study activities are not like what goes on in a fast-food restaurant. We go to the meeting; we listen to the teacher or preacher; we quickly get it all down in correct outlines; and then we rush off to something else. We do not take time to think, ponder, question, reflect, relate, or apply. The sad result is a great gap between learning and living.

Our brothers and sisters in Canada and Great Britain have a wonderful custom that at least illustrates what I am concerned about. (I'm not saying that everyone who follows this custom necessarily benefits from it, but that does not minimize its value.) When the sermon is over and the congregation has sung the final hymn and received the benediction, *the congregation sits down and lets the impact of the service sink in.* There is a time of quiet meditation. I have noted, too, that even after some worshipers start to leave, others remain seated and continue to think on the Word.

Whether we like it or not, it takes time to be holy. Too many of us are caught up in the evangelical rat race, and we simply do not take time to digest the Word of God. We are proud of our libraries, our outlines, our cassettes, and our record of attendance at services and seminars; but are we proud of the results? Are we cultivating a fast-food faith when we should be taking time to be holy?

One summer, some physical problems forced me to cancel several meetings and to stay home and rest. I had a three-week enforced vacation, and it was one of the best things that ever happened to me. In between resting, taking medication, and visiting two different doctors, I had time to read, to think, to pray over the Word of God. Believe me, I have always been faithful in my daily devotional time; but this experience was different. God slowed me down so that I could digest some of the spiritual food he had shared with me.

I wonder if we may be cramming too much activity into our church programs and into our worship services. Are we giving people time to meditate? Do we really need ten minutes of announcements and promotion? (I often wonder what church bulletins are for!) Must we rush from meeting to meeting like people who are haunted by the fear that, if we stop, we may fall apart?

You may have heard about the explorer who was penetrating a difficult area of the jungle and wanted to keep going, but his native bearers would not move. "We have been going too fast," they explained, "and we must wait here for our souls to catch up with our bodies." Not a bad reason for sitting still!

There is a subtle danger in cramming ourselves full of Bible knowledge that never really gets into our inner person. We start equating knowledge with spirituality, and activity with ministry; and then we start living on substitutes. Manton also said, "The end of study is information, and the need of meditation is practice." He is right. Knowing Bible facts is not the same as receiving Bible truths and making them a vital part of our inner person.

You and I may not be able to control all that goes on in church services, but we can control what we do with what we learn. (I suppose if I sat and meditated at the close of the service in the average church, the custodian would tiptoe up and ask if I were sick.) What would happen to our practical Christian walk if we drove home from church in quiet meditation instead of listening to the car radio or a new music cassette? Or if we spent a few minutes at home alone with the Lord instead of immediately turning on the television or picking up the newspaper?

Radical? Perhaps; but the malady is so serious that we need radical measures! Even the secular world is promoting all kinds of "meditation," and harassed people are paying hundreds of dollars just to learn how to sit and be quiet and think. The blessed man described in Psalm 1 took the Bible seriously and meditated on its truths day and night. The word *meditate* is used seven times in Psalm 119, and it is usually connected with delighting in the Word or loving the Word.

"This Book of the Law shall not depart from your mouth," the Lord said to Joshua, "but thou shalt meditate in it day and night [for what purpose?], that you may observe to do according to all that is written in it" (Josh. 1:8). The bridge between learning and living is meditating—praying over the Word, pondering it, applying it to our own lives.

This is the only sure way to spiritual prosperity and success.

10 THE POWER SOURCE

When some American visitors asked Charles Haddon Spurgeon the secret of his ministry, the great preacher quietly replied, "My people pray for me."

No doubt other factors were involved in Spurgeon's success. He was a devoted student of the Scriptures, a gifted speaker, and a man totally committed to the ministry of the Word. God had chosen him to accomplish a singular ministry, and Spurgeon was conscious of this divine calling. But all of these factors, apart from prayer, would have contributed very little.

"The minister who does not earnestly pray over his work must surely be a vain and conceited man," Spurgeon told his ministerial students. "He acts as if he thought himself sufficient of himself, and therefore needed not to appeal to God."

In his sermon on "Peter's Shortest Prayer" ("Lord, save me!"), Spurgeon said, "I always feel that there is something wrong if I go without prayer for even half an hour in the day." He lived and labored in constant communion with God, and his ministry continues to bear fruit.

But it is also true that his people did pray for him. While Spurgeon was proclaiming the Word in the great Metropolitan Tabernacle, hundreds of his members would be gathered in prayer in a lower auditorium. I have no doubt that hundreds more were praying even as they listened to him preach.

I would encourage believers today to pray for pastors and others who minister the Word of God. It is only as we pray that the power of God will be revealed in their ministry. For some reason, we feel that a man's academic excellence or his wide experience will guarantee spiritual success; so we neglect to pray. How foolish we are!

Certainly we ought to pray for our ministers as they study the Word and prepare their messages. Said Spurgeon, "Texts will often refuse to reveal their treasure 'till you open them with the key of prayer." It is the prayer support of God's people that turns the pastor's study into a powerhouse. The sermon will be only so much dry tinder unless it is kindled by believing prayer.

We ought also to pray for the minister as he delivers the Word. Those of us who preach know that preaching is an exacting experience that demands the very best of us. One of my professors at seminary claimed that an earnest preacher expended in thirty minutes the energy spent by an average laborer in eight hours. That is a lot of energy! And when you add to this the constant attacks of Satan, it is not difficult to conclude that the preacher needs prayer support as he delivers the Word.

But even apart from his preaching ministry, the pastor desperately needs prayer help. For one thing, the servant of God is susceptible to pressures and trials that most church members know nothing about. The church member can turn to his pastor for help in life's problems. To whom does the pastor turn? Where does he find strength and encouragement when the going is difficult? Knowing that his people pray for him and seeing the answers to their prayers in his own life is the greatest encouragement in the world.

The servant of God also needs prayer for his family. If only church members prayed for the pastor's family as much as they criticize them! When people have told me, "We pray for you and your family," I have been greatly helped. No pastor's wife and children are perfect. (In this, they resemble the other wives and children in the congregation.) In a minister's home, there are demands and sacrifices that may not be present in the homes of other church members. It is only as we pray that these demands will be met and the Lord glorified.

A praying pastor and a praying people are a powerful combination. No doubt Satan will do everything he can to hinder such a ministry, and we must even pray about that! The spiritual weapon of "all prayer" (Eph. 6:18) is one that Satan cannot overcome.

Before we begin special times of prayer in the church (as important as they are), we need to strengthen the regular prayer meetings. It does us little good to assemble wearily at six o'clock Saturday morning if we cannot assemble enthusiastically at seven o'clock Wednesday evening. If a church would seek revival blessings, let the pastor and people first make good use of the stated times of prayer; and then the Spirit will direct concerning special intercession meetings. After all, a change of schedule can never bring a change in character or ministry. We must start where we are.

The great need of the church today is intercessory prayer. We need praying pastors and praying people. We need people who will pray specifically and not try to salve their consciences with "Lord, bless the church." We need Christians who are not ashamed to pray or to ask for prayer. After all, if the great apostle Paul admitted his need for prayer, where does that leave the rest of us? The fact that we do not sense our need for prayer is in itself evidence that we are far needier than we think.

"Beloved brethren," said Spurgeon to his ministerial students, "let us pray. We cannot all argue, but we can all pray; we cannot all be leaders, but we can all be pleaders; we cannot all be mighty in rhetoric, but we can all be prevalent in prayer. I would sooner see you eloquent with God than with men."

If each believer who reads these words will examine his or her own prayer life and will determine, with God's help, to be faithful in prayer, we will see the power of God at work in our churches, homes, and individual lives. If we will faithfully pray for those in authority, we will see God do mighty things in the nations of the world. The crying need of the hour is for men and women of prayer.

Will you be among them?

11 WINNING YOUR WINGS

*O*n a moment of desperation and discouragement, King David said: "Oh that I had wings like a dove! for then would I fly away, and be at rest" (Ps. 55:6 KJV).

We don't criticize David for honestly expressing his despair and wanting to get away from it all. All of us have shared the same feelings at one time or another. But we have learned that we can't run away from life's burdens and problems.

In short, when it comes to the problems of life, expect them, enlist them, and encounter them victoriously through faith in God. Don't fly away from the storms; fly above the storms. Instead of asking God for wings like a dove's so you can escape, ask him for wings like the eagle's! "But they that wait upon the LORD shall renew their strength; they shall mount up with wings as eagles" (Isa. 40:31 KJV).

When we find ourselves in a difficult situation, most of us pray, "Father, get me out of this!" If nothing happens immediately, then we pray, "Father, *when* will I get out of this?" But what we ought to be praying is, "Father, *what* should I get out of this?" There is a purpose in trials, and even discouraging days can be excellent teachers of spiritual lessons that we could learn no other way.

"The troubles of my heart are enlarged: O bring thou me out of my distresses" (Ps. 25:17 KJV). Enlarged troubles! David was going through an especially trying time and desperately needed God's direction and deliverance. It's likely that Psalm 25 was written during the period when Saul was persecuting David and trying to kill him.

Why does God permit "enlarged troubles"? Surely our Father in heaven would want his children to be comfortable and free from afflictions. Not so! God has never promised to make us comfortable, but he has promised to make us *conformable*. Our Father's purpose is that all of his children "be conformed to the image of his Son" (Rom. 8:29 KJV); and in order to conform us, he must permit us to suffer. Even our Lord Jesus learned obedience through suffering.

But "enlarged troubles" are but the beginning. There is a second step in this process: "Thou hast enlarged me when I was in distress" (Ps. 4:1 KJV).

Enlarged troubles can produce enlarged saints! I say *"can* produce" because troubles don't automatically produce giants. I've seen Christians go through the furnace and come out midgets—small in outlook, small in faith, and small in ministry. King Saul and King David illustrate these opposite effects of trials. Saul was a big man physically but a midget spiritually, and his experiences in battle only made him smaller. We have no evidence that David was a big man physically, but he was certainly a spiritual giant. How did he get that way? Enlarged troubles made him an enlarged saint *because he trusted God.*

How we respond to the difficulties of life helps to determine how long our Father will permit them to continue. When your Father permits you to go into the furnace of affliction, he always keeps his eye on the clock and his hand on the thermostat. He knows how much you can take and how long the trial should be. But he watches us to see if the trials are accomplishing all that they should accomplish.

Enlarged troubles can lead to enlarged saints. What's the next step? "He brought me forth also into a large place" (Ps. 18:19 KJV). God uses enlarged trials to produce enlarged saints so he can put them into enlarged places!

All of God's giants have been men and women who have experienced suffering in one way or another. Joseph spent thirteen years as a forgotten servant—even a prisoner—because God was getting him ready for a bigger place. God must prepare us for what he prepares for us, and a part of that preparation is the furnace of affliction.

Now we can better understand why David had to experience so many storms: God had chosen him to fill a big place, and David had to be enlarged. Had David gotten his request for "wings like a dove" and flown away from the storm, he would have wasted all that suffering and still been unprepared for his great opportunities to serve God. Instead of getting "wings like a dove," he received "wings like an eagle" and flew right into the face of the storm and triumphed over it.

But one more step remains: "Thou hast enlarged my steps under me, that my feet did not slip" (Ps. 18:36 KJV).

An enlarged place can be a dangerous place if we don't know how to take giant steps of faith and walk with God. David's feet did not slip as Saul's did, because David had grown during those years of trial; and David knew how to take giant steps of commitment to God.

If you plan to walk by faith, then you must learn to take giant steps, and this means you must expect difficulties. The nation of Israel failed to claim its inheritance because of unbelief. An entire generation wasted their years of suffering in Egypt! The new generation needed the discipline of the wilderness to enlarge them for their enlarged privileges and responsibilities. At the close of their forty years of learning to trust God, the new generation was ready and eager to conquer Canaan and claim their inheritance.

They were bigger people, prepared for a bigger place!

There is simply no breaking this divine principle. If you want to take giant steps in an enlarged place, then you must become an enlarged person; and this can be done only as you trust God in the midst of enlarged trials. There are no ninety-day wonders among God's giants. All of them won their wings the hard way. You and I may never have seen the trials they endured; but God saw them, and God used them to accomplish his great purposes.

It appears, then, that one of the most important things in our Christian life is that we win our wings. There are no honorary awards in the battles of life; you have to win your wings. The quitter gets "wings like a dove," but the winner gets "wings like an eagle."

But let me add a special word of encouragement: *Nobody need fail permanently*. Even David tried to escape on his own, but this didn't completely disqualify him. God disciplined him and brought him back to the place of obedience, and David won his wings.

Some of the most successful preachers I know were anything but a success when they first began their ministry, and some of them would admit they seriously considered quitting. But God gave them their wings, and they learned how to soar above the storms and make the wind work for them rather than against them. Now they are telling others how to win their wings.

Start winning your wings!

God has many "enlarged places" in this world that desperately need to be filled. He is looking for enlarged saints.

Will you be one of them?

12 THE FURNACES OF LIFE

*E*verybody at one time or another must go through experiences of trial and testing. This is one of the facts of life that we had better accept if we intend to make circumstances our servants and not our masters.

We picture these difficult times in different ways. "I'm really going through a battle!" we might say to a trusted friend. Or we could say, "Our family is in the middle of a storm."

But one of the most vivid images of testings and trials is that of the furnace. "The refining pot is for silver and the furnace for gold, but the LORD tests the hearts" (Prov. 17:3). Wealthy Solomon knew something about gold and silver, but he also knew something about life. He knew that God sometimes puts his people into the furnace in order to prove them and to purify them.

Let's review some of the furnaces of life and receive from the Lord the encouragement we need for these demanding days.

The Furnace of Pain

"But [God] knows the way that I take," said Job from his ash heap. "When He has tested me, I shall come forth as gold" (23:10).

Next to our Lord Jesus Christ, perhaps no man mentioned in the Bible suffered more than Job. First he lost his wealth, then his children, then his health, and then the encouragement of his wife and his friends. He sat alone on his ash heap, listening to his friends falsely diagnose his case and try to prove that he was a secret sinner who was being punished by God.

Their theory, of course, was that God always blesses the righteous with health and wealth but punishes the wicked by making them suffer.

Now, God does sometimes use physical suffering to discipline his children. But this does not mean that every case of suffering in the family of God is necessarily a punishment from God. It may be that God has other purposes in mind when he permits us to go into the furnace of pain. Joseph suffered in various ways for thirteen years, yet he was certainly not in the furnace because of disobedience to God. The prophet Jeremiah and the apostle Paul both suffered greatly, yet their suffering came because they obeyed God, not because they disobeyed him.

Job understood the furnace of pain. God was purging away the dross so that Job might come out of the furnace as pure gold.

None of us enjoys pain. The furnace of pain is not something that we pray for or eagerly anticipate, but sometimes we need it. Like Job, we must enter the furnace by faith and trust the Father to accomplish his purposes in our life. It is better to go through the furnace and come out as pure gold than to be too cheap to be useful in the hands of the Father.

The Furnace of Praise

"The refining pot is for silver and the furnace for gold, and a man is valued by what others say of him" (Prov. 27:21).

This simple proverb is quite broad in its interpretation and application. For one thing, it warns us not to believe all the complimentary things people say about us. "You had better put people's praise into the furnace," warned Solomon, "and get rid of the dross. Otherwise, you might start believing what they say, and this can lead to pride and sin."

This proverb also says that people are tested and proved by what they praise. That makes good sense. Persons who praise a crafty politician for lying his way out of trouble simply announce to the world that they themselves are liars.

But there is another interpretation and application of this proverb: How people respond to praise tests their true character. In other words, praise is like a furnace—it can bring out either the best in us or the worst in us.

Saul and David come to mind. When they returned from their battles, they were met by adoring crowds who praised them. "Saul has slain his thousands," they sang, "and David his ten thousands!" David responded to that song by being humble and submissive, walking carefully before the people and the Lord. Saul responded by envying David and then trying to kill him. Saul ended up a suicide on the battlefield, while David went on to prosper and to reign.

The way we respond to criticism depends on the way we respond to praise. If praise humbles us, then criticism will build us up. But if praise inflates us, then criticism will crush us; and both responses lead to defeat.

D. Martyn Lloyd-Jones used to warn young preachers, "It is a sad thing when a man succeeds before he is ready for it."

I have noticed that the Christians who really have something to brag about rarely brag. They are content to let God review their record and grant the reward. These people have been tested in the furnace of praise and have come out pure gold to the glory of God.

The Furnace of Persecution

"Beloved, do not think it strange concerning the fiery trial which is to try [test] you, as though some strange thing happened to you" (1 Pet. 4:12).

"That the genuineness of your faith, being much more precious than gold that perishes, though it is tried with fire, may be found to praise, honor, and glory at the revelation of Jesus Christ" (1:7).

Peter knew what he was writing about. From the beginning of his ministry he was faced with persecution. Nor was he surprised when it came; for, after all, didn't the Lord prepare the disciples for the furnace of persecution? "In the world you will have tribulation; but be of good cheer, I have overcome the world" (John 16:33). The more we live like the Lord Jesus Christ, the more we can expect to be treated the way he was treated. "Yes, and all who desire to live godly in Christ Jesus will suffer persecution" (2 Tim. 3:12).

When the believer faces the furnace of persecution, it is actually a compliment. Woe unto that Christian who gets along with the world and wins the world's praises! Shadrach, Meshach, and Abednego could have conformed to the king's will and avoided the furnace, but they preferred to obey the Lord.

"God examineth with trials," said the Puritan Henry Smith, "the devil examineth with temptations, the world examineth with persecutions." The furnace of persecution is evidence that the believer is creating problems for the world, and the world cannot take it. "If the world hates you," Jesus told his disciples, "you know that it hated Me before it hated you" (John 15:18).

But Peter tells us that the furnace of persecution brings more benefits than it does burdens, no matter how difficult it may be to experience. For one thing, we are suffering for the sake of the Lord Jesus, and that is a privilege. "For to you has been granted on behalf of Christ, not only to believe in Him, but also to suffer for His sake" (Phil. 1:29). It is a grand thing to be identified with "the fellowship of His sufferings" (3:10)!

God does not always settle his accounts immediately. The world persecutes the church and often appears to be the victor in the battle; but one day, God will judge the world and glorify the church. In the life of the faithful Christian, God can transform suffering into glory, persecution into coronation.

The Furnace of Punishment

It is a remarkable thing that our Lord, while on earth, said more about hell than he did about heaven. He compares hell to the garbage dump, Gehenna, that was located outside Jerusalem, "where 'their worm does not die, and the fire is not quenched'" (Mark 9:44). He also compares hell to outer darkness (see Matt. 8:12; 22:13; 25:30), a horrible place away from the presence of God, who is light.

"There is no hell!" says the liberal theologian. "A God of love would not send people to a furnace of eternal fire!" But God does not send people to hell; they send themselves. Hell was prepared for Satan and his angels, not for people made in God's image. Those who follow Satan and believe his lies must end up where he ends up—in hell.

Hell might be considered a monstrous blot against the holy character of God were it not for Calvary. God has prepared a way for sinners to escape the furnace of fire, and that way is his Son, Jesus Christ. He endured the fire of hell for a lost world. He went through the outer darkness. He identified himself with the sins of the world—yes, was made sin for us—so that we might be saved from eternal judgment.

Because there is such a place as hell, it behooves us who are saved to warn a lost world of the wrath to come. It was said of D. L. Moody that he never mentioned hell in his sermons without a tear in his eye. God has sent us out to be witnesses, not prosecuting attorneys. Let's not act as though we are glad people are going to hell. Let's do something to stop them!

God's children experience furnaces and must go through the fire, but we will never experience the furnace of eternal punishment. "There is therefore now no condemnation to those who are in Christ Jesus" (Rom. 8:1).

Let's not be afraid of the furnaces of life, for God is in control and is working out his wonderful purposes. Rather, let's fear lest we fail to witness, pray, and give as we should so that others might escape the furnace of hell.

If you have never trusted Christ, then receive him now. He is the only Savior, and the only way he will save you is by your trusting him and opening your life to him. "But as many as received [Christ], to them He gave the right to become children of God, even to those who believe in His name" (John 1:12).

13 WE'RE A BUNCH OF "ONE-PERSONS"

*O*n a society that puts too much emphasis on numbers, we tend to forget the importance of the individual. And yet, it is the individual—that one man or woman—who ultimately must get the job done.

Bible history is filled with examples of this principle. When God wanted to redeem a lost world, he called Abraham and Sarah—two individuals—and set in motion his great plan that culminated in the birth of Jesus Christ. When God wanted to redeem the Israelites from bondage, he did not call a committee meeting. He called one man—Moses—and used him to free the people. When the time came for the Israelites to claim their inheritance, God had his leader ready—Joshua, the son of Nun.

To be sure, no one person can do the whole job. Those individuals who labor with a great leader who has been raised up by God are also important. They may not be publicly recognized, but their service for God makes them important. In other words, it is individuals who get the job done, whether as leaders or followers. God cannot do without the individual.

We hear a great deal about large, "super-aggressive" churches these days, and if they give a true witness, we are grateful for them. But churches are made up of individuals, and it is the individual and not the whole congregation who is getting the job done. This means that the personal witness of the member in the smaller church is just as important as any individual in the larger church. In fact, it may be more important since, in the smaller church, there are fewer available to do the job.

One fallacy of organizational work is the idea that once a group has made a decision, the matter is settled and successful. Not so! Congress can pass a law, but the mere passing of that law will never change anything. Somebody must set the wheels in motion to enforce the law, and this is where the individual becomes important. A local church can vote to adopt a program of evangelism, but that will not make it a soul-winning church. The plan must be expedited, and only individuals can do that.

Never underestimate the influence of one person. Mary of Bethany brought her offering to her Lord in the privacy of a home, and yet Jesus said that her act of worship would have spiritual influence around the world (see Mark 14:9). Your private prayer time, your personal worship, is important to the work of God around the world. The smallest local congregation has a vital part to play in the worldwide program of redemption.

I fear that our constant emphasis on bigness and greatness may be giving some saints an inferiority complex. I hear of church members deserting their neighborhood churches in order to flock to the larger churches where "things are happening." These people may feel more important, but perhaps their greatest opportunities were left behind them in a place that needed them desperately.

In my travels, I meet pastors who are ready to quit because they do not seem to be accomplishing much. "I pastor a small church" is the way they often introduce themselves, and I usually reply, "There are no small churches and there are no big preachers! Wherever Christ is honored and the Word faithfully preached, that is a big and an important place." The greatest job in the world is the task he has given you to do. Stick with it!

Nobody knows the name of that layman whose stammering sermon led young Charles Haddon Spurgeon to Christ, but the consequences were tremendous. I am sure that substitute preacher went home after the service and lamented the fact that he had ever tried to preach. Yet God used an individual to touch another individual, and that second individual was used of God to influence the whole world. Keep preaching the Word, my brother! Keep teaching the Word, my sister! You are important in the work of God, and your labor will not be in vain.

Nobody will dispute the fact that we want to reach as many as possible with the Good News of salvation. The early church managed to get the job done without any of the modern means of transportation and communication that we can enlist for the gospel today. How did they do it? By individuals witnessing to individuals. We read in the Book of the Acts about Peter and Paul and their sermons to the multitudes, but we also read about multitudes of unnamed saints who simply went from place to place "gossiping the gospel." Church historians remind us that the Roman Empire was conquered for Christ, not only by the endeavors of the great missionaries and apostles but also by the daily witness of the individual believers.

Well, we are back where we started—the importance of the individual. That means *you*. God has an important place for you to fill, an important job for you to accomplish. Your name may never appear in a magazine or book or, for that matter, in the church bulletin. But God will keep the records and give the rewards. Your responsibility is to be faithful, and your privilege is to glorify and please him.

As Edward Everett Hale once said, "I am only one, but still I am one. I cannot do everything, but still I can do something. And because I cannot do everything I will not refuse to do the something that I can do." If God has called me to do it, then what I do is important to him and to the ministry of the church. It matters not who gets the credit as long as God gets the glory. What I do is important, not because I am doing it but because God has called me to do it. There will be temptations to stoop to lesser things, but I must resist them. Like Nehemiah, I must say, "I am doing a great work, so that I cannot come down" (see Neh. 6:3). Whatever God calls me to do is the most important task at hand, and I must do it.

Will you join me?

14 WANTED: HINGE PEOPLE

*H*ere is a list of men who played an important role in the work of God. How many of them are familiar to you?

A. M. Poindexter

John Rough and William Pulsford

Arthur Rust, Cecil Hodges, and Frank Wimpory

J. W. T. Dewhirst, George Gould, and Thomas Olney

If none of these names are familiar to you, don't despair. They were unfamiliar to me until I began to investigate the lives of the great preachers. My purpose was this: I wanted to learn if there were unknown people in the lives of these men who were important to their ministry. Let me illustrate what I mean.

Every student of church history knows that John Knox was the dedicated leader of the Reformation in Scotland. But many people don't realize that it was John Rough who persuaded Knox to give up his work as a teacher and to enter into the work of the church. Rough urged Knox to help him in his preaching ministry; and at the close of one of his sermons, Rough ended the message by looking squarely at Knox and publicly charging him to take up the work.

John Rough was what I call a "hinge person." Just as a large door can swing on a small hinge, so a great life can be guided by a perhaps seemingly insignificant event or a little-known person. The great people of history owe much to these hinge people.

Who was George Gould? He was a British Christian who lived in Loughton and one day heard a young preacher address a Sunday-school meeting in Cambridge. He was so impressed with the young preacher that he mentioned his name to his London friend, Thomas Olney. Olney was a deacon at a London church that was seeking a new pastor, so he arranged for the young man to come to preach. And that was how Charles Haddon Spurgeon happened to be called to the New Park Street Chapel in London. George Gould was the hinge person on which that door turned, and we all know the results as God blessed Spurgeon's ministry in London.

John Henry Jowett was called "the greatest preacher in the English-speaking world"—and perhaps he was. But he didn't start out to be a preacher; his goal was law and perhaps Parliament. The day before he was to sign the papers that would open the door to his training in law, he "happened" to meet his Sunday-school teacher, J. W. T. Dewhirst. Jowett eagerly told him about his plans, and Dewhirst quietly replied, "I had always hoped you would enter the ministry." Jowett changed his plans.

In his early ministry F. B. Meyer was discouraged because of opposition in the church he was pastoring. The officers didn't approve of Meyer's evangelistic emphasis or his concern for the neglected people in Leicester. Finally, Meyer resigned from the church and accepted a call to a church in Sheffield. He was on his way to the post office to mail his letter of acceptance when he met Arthur Rust. He told Rust about his plans, and Rust informed Meyer of *his* plans! Rust and a group of Christian businessmen in

Leicester had met together a few days before, burdened to begin a church ministry in Leicester that would reach the masses and spread the gospel. Since this was Meyer's burden, why couldn't he become their pastor? That was the beginning of the amazing ministry of Melbourne Hall, and it came about because of a "chance meeting" at the post office. Arthur Rust was the hinge person God used to open the door.

The next time you sing "O Love That Wilt Not Let Me Go," try to remember that the man who wrote the words—blind George Matheson—was influenced toward the ministry by a man he met but once, William Pulsford. In fact, Pulsford himself didn't know he had even touched Matheson's life until Pulsford was on his deathbed.

William Pulsford was the godly pastor of Trinity Church in Glasgow when Matheson was a student there. "The man of all others that shaped my personality was Pulsford," said Matheson. "I never heard a man who so inspired me. He set me on fire and, under God, was my spiritual creator." And yet in his day, William Pulsford was not considered a popular preacher or even an especially gifted pulpiteer; but God used him as a hinge person to direct the life of a man whose ministry blessed thousands—and continues to bless.

When I was a ministerial student, our textbook for preaching class was the famous *On the Preparation and Delivery of Sermons*, by John A. Broadus. Broadus is still recognized as one of the greatest teachers of preachers in American church history, and his books are still used in the classrooms of our seminaries.

But John Broadus wanted to be a doctor! One day he heard A. M. Poindexter preach a sermon on the parable of the talents, and he felt God's call to the ministry. Poindexter's name is not as famous as that of Broadus, but his ministry was important. He was a hinge person that God used to accomplish his purposes. Many preachers join me in thanking God for the ministry of John A. Broadus.

The important thing now is to gather some practical lessons from these examples.

The first lesson is obvious: *all believers are important to God and his work.* Recently I purchased a copy of William Sangster's book *The Pure in Heart,* and I reflected on the life of that great Methodist preacher. I then checked his biography to see if there were some hinge people in his life—and sure enough, there were: Cecil Hodges and Frank Wimpory. It was Hodges who invited young Sangster to attend the Radnor Street Mission in London, and it was Wimpory who sensed that the lad was under conviction and led him to trust in Christ.

There are no small people in the kingdom of God as far as our Father is concerned. Not everybody will become a Spurgeon or a Jowett or a Sangster, but anybody can be used of God to open the door for others to become effective in the service of Christ. I wonder how many faithful Sunday-school teachers have been hinge persons and have led to Christ students who later became effective servants of God. It was Edward Kimball, a modest Sunday-school teacher, who claimed D. L. Moody for Christ; and Moody's ministry still blesses the world.

These hinge people I have named probably had no idea that their words and ministries would have such tremendous results, but God knew that blessings were in store. The important thing is to be faithful and do the job—God will do the rest. The next time you feel like resigning, just remind yourself, "There may be a future D. L. Moody in my class!" You might be a hinge person and not know it.

Not only are all believers important to God, but *all contacts and ministries are important to God.* There are no accidents with God, only appointments. I believe in the providence of God, and this confidence encourages me in my ministry. You never know how God might use even a casual contact to influence and direct a person's life.

This means that you and I must be "prayed up" and walking in the Spirit each day of our lives. We must ask God to guide us even in the seemingly insignificant events of life. I went to a birthday party one day, and that social event became a spiritual event for me. A friend who was there made a suggestion to me, and as a result, I attended a certain school. It was there that I met my wife and was trained in the special way that God wanted me to be trained. And it all started with a birthday party.

This doesn't mean, of course, that we must treat every event or decision as though it is a turning point in our lives. If we did, we would lose our balance and perspective. In 1 Corinthians 10:27, Paul suggests that it isn't necessary to fast and pray over every social invitation we receive; but we still must be alert to what the Lord may be saying to us in the everyday contacts of life. This comes from walking in the Spirit and keeping in touch with the Lord.

The hinge people that God uses certainly get their special reward, even though they may not be recognized and applauded. The important thing is that we accomplish God's will, not that we become famous. One day in heaven we will discover how God used us to help mold and direct the lives of others. Today we may be discouraged and think our work is futile, but when we see Christ, we will praise him for what he did.

So let's live in the light of that praise today. Let's pull ourselves out of the slough of despond by reminding ourselves that God is doing far more than we realize and that our "labor is not in vain in the Lord." We may not be the great door that is seen by others, but we can be the hinge people that help the door to move.

15 FOUR FAMILIAR FALLACIES

*L*et me share with you four familiar fallacies relating to the will of God.

The first is: *The will of God is dangerous.* "I would surrender to the Lord," says a trembling believer, "but I'm afraid of what might happen!" Over the centuries, the adversary has convinced God's people that the will of God is distasteful instead of delightful and dangerous instead of safe. We approach praying about God's will (*if* we pray at all) in the same way we approach a visit to the doctor. We anxiously ask, "I wonder what I will find out—and where it will lead?"

The truly surrendered saint knows that the safest place in the world is in the will of God. Instead of asking, "What will happen if I obey God's will?" we should be asking, "What will happen if I disobey God's will?" Jonah disobeyed God's will and created problems both for himself and those on ship with him. David disobeyed God's will and brought judgment to his family and his nation.

How can the will of God be dangerous when the will of God is the expression of the love of God? "The counsel of the LORD standeth for ever," says Psalm 33:11, "the thoughts of his heart to all generations." The will of God comes from the heart of God, and whatever comes from God's heart certainly cannot be dangerous.

Granted, in obeying God's will, we might find ourselves in hard places, going through trying circumstances. But God is with us! The grace of God will surely sustain us where the will of God has led us. The test of spiritual Christian living is not how much trouble we can escape but whether or not we are glorifying God in every circumstance of life.

A second fallacy states that *the will of God is distant.* In other words, don't be concerned about God's will today. It's the big future things you need to pray about—what school to attend, what job to accept, what person you should marry, where you should retire, and so on. Of course, the weakness of this attitude toward the will of God is that it separates the present from the future, and this is impossible to do. If I expect to be in God's will tomorrow, I had better be in God's will today. A life spent in God's will is made up of days and hours lived in God's will.

Perhaps I need to illustrate this truth. When a rocket is launched from Cape Kennedy, it has to be on target. If the rocket is but one degree off course a thousand feet off the launching pad, that one degree may become ten degrees as it moves into space. Scientists have developed control rockets that keep spacecraft on course.

While it is important to pray about future decisions, it is also important to seek God's will about decisions today. A Christian dare not postpone the will of God. It is something we all must live with each day. If our hearts are right with the Father, we have no problem living with and in the will of God. To ignore God's will today and yet plan to do God's will tomorrow is the height of folly. It reminds me of the pilot who announced to the passengers in the plane, "We're lost, but we're making very good time."

The idea that *God's will is divided* is another fallacy that has led believers into disobedience and disappointment. Many Christians have the strange notion that the will of God is something like a mail-order catalog: You can select Good or Better or Best. The only difference is in the price that you pay. If you want the best, you have to pay for it.

Perhaps this fallacy has arisen from a misunderstanding of Romans 12:2, where Paul stated, "That you may prove what is that good and acceptable and perfect will of God." A believer once said to me, "I guess I don't want God's perfect will for my life, but I'll settle for his good will." But God does not have three wills for my life. He has one will, and that will is good and acceptable and perfect. God does not hand us an order blank and ask us to check whether or not we want his "good will," his "acceptable will" or his "perfect will." Because he is God, he can only will that which is best for us. For him to will anything else would be impossible, for he is the unchanging God.

The word translated "prove" in Romans 12:2 means "to prove by experience." As we obey the will of God, we discover that it is good for us. The more we obey, the better God's will becomes to us until it is not simply "acceptable" (which means "well-pleasing") but perfect. We would not accept a substitute.

Perhaps the greatest fallacy of all is that *God's will is difficult to discover*. When I was a child at home, I had little difficulty learning what my parents wanted me to do. When I became a father, I tried to communicate my will to our children. Why would our heavenly Father deliberately hide his will from his blood-bought children? Why would he make it difficult for us to know his plans for our lives?

To be sure, God has his times as well as his purposes. You and I need to mature spiritually if we would enter into the secrets of the Lord. But that is a far different thing from discerning God's will about the decisions of life. My guess is that God's children are not serious enough about God's will, and this is why he remains silent. Or perhaps we pray about things that have already been settled and are clearly revealed in the Bible. Most of the decisions we make in daily life can be guided by the precepts, promises, or principles found in the Bible. The better we know the Word of God, the better we will know the will of God.

A willingness to obey God's will is essential for knowing God's will. Jesus made this clear in John 7:17. God is willing to guide us if we are willing to follow. It has been my experience—both through success and failure—that God is more willing to reveal his plans to me than I am to obey them. He knows when we are serious about knowing his will and doing it.

It is not important that we always understand God's will. We do not live by explanations; we live by promises. The giants of faith named in Hebrews 11 did not always understand the divine plan, but they were blessed in doing it. And after all, that is the purpose of God's will for our lives—that we might receive his blessing, learn to enjoy it, and then share it with others. The more we enjoy the will of God, the better we will be able to discover it and do it.

Beware of these four familiar fallacies. They always lead to defeat, and after all, defeat for a Christian is simply missing the will of God and settling for a cheap substitute.

16 NOTHING BUT MANNA?

*J*ust as each stage of physical growth has its own peculiar dangers and problems, so the different stages of spiritual growth present hazards and challenges. The younger Christian is zealous for the Lord but may lack spiritual knowledge. The older believer has a great deal of knowledge, but his zeal may have grown cold.

I have felt for a long time that one of the particular temptations of the maturing Christian is the danger of getting accustomed to his blessings. Like the world traveler who has been everywhere and seen everything, the maturing Christian is in danger of taking his blessings for granted and getting so accustomed to them that they fail to excite him as they once did.

Emerson said that if the stars came out only once a year, everybody would stay up all night to behold them. We have seen the stars so often that we don't bother to look at them anymore. We have grown accustomed to our blessings.

The Israelites in the wilderness got accustomed to their blessings, and God had to chasten the people (see Num. 11). God had fed the nation with heavenly manna each morning, and yet the people were getting tired of it. "But now our whole being is dried up," they said, "there is nothing at all except this manna before our eyes!" (v. 6).

Nothing but manna! They were experiencing a miracle of God's provision every morning; yet they were no longer excited about it. Nothing but manna!

One of the evidences that we have grown accustomed to our blessings is this spirit of criticism and complaining. Instead of thanking God for what we have, we complain about it and tell him we wish we had something else. You can be sure that if God *did* give us what we asked for, we would eventually complain about that. The person who has gotten accustomed to his blessings can never be satisfied.

Another evidence of this malady is the idea that others have a better situation than we do. The Israelites remembered their diet in Egypt and longed to return to the cucumbers, melons, leeks, onions, and garlic. They were saying, "The people in Egypt are so much better off than we are!" Obviously, they had forgotten the slavery they had endured in Egypt and the terrible bondage from which God had delivered them. Slavery is a high price to pay for a change in diet.

When I was in the pastorate, I heard my share of criticism from church members. I always listened to honest, sincere criticism and tried to profit from it, but I paid little attention to the "wilderness grumblings" of the disgruntled saints who had gotten accustomed to their blessings. In fact, sometimes I even suggested that they pray about attending another church for a time, just to see if their criticisms were valid. They usually came back in a chastened mood.

In our families, our children go through this grumbling stage, usually early in adolescence. Their key word is "tired"—they are tired of the old house, tired of the old car, tired of the same old food, tired of the same old church, and so on. Each of their friends has a better house or car, a better church, and enjoys better food. Of course, parents are hurt by this kind of talk, but they love the children anyway and patiently wait for them to grow up.

Each local church has its share of members who have itching ears and who run here and there to hear some new thing. Then they return to church in order to contrast their pastor with a preacher they have heard, the choir with a professional singing group, and the youth ministry with the program their teenagers were in at a summer conference. Instead of being thankful to God for what they have, they complain about what they don't have.

I believe God is grieved when we get accustomed to our blessings and start to complain and criticize. The record in Numbers 11 tells us that even Moses became discouraged and wanted to die. I wonder how many pastors, Sunday-school teachers, and choir members have resigned because of the constant complaining of believers who got accustomed to their blessings. God chastened the Israelites because of their complaining. He gave them the flesh that they begged for, but this flesh brought death. They would have been better off to have settled for the manna! "And He gave them their request, but sent leanness into their soul" (Ps. 106:15).

The best cure for the sin of getting accustomed to our blessings is this: Constantly give thanks to God for all he gives and all he does. A thankful heart, lost in the wonder of God's grace and goodness, will never take God's blessings for granted. Just as a little child is constantly filled with wonder at what life brings him, so the maturing believer must marvel at God's gifts and God's provisions. Why should God bless us? Who are we that God should care for us?

In the final analysis, it is pride that makes us accustomed to our blessings. We forget that we have been saved by grace, not by our own merit, and that it is of the Lord's mercies that we are not consumed. Pride leads to complaining and criticizing, and pride leads to a fall.

Beware of getting accustomed to your blessings.

17 THE FACT WE DARE NOT IGNORE

The famous agnostic lawyer Clarence Darrow once called the celebration of Christmas "a humbug, a public nuisance." He said, "People would be better off if they paid no attention to it."

To be sure, a person could ignore the celebration of our Lord's birth. Each December, millions of people do it, just as each year millions of Christians ignore the celebrations held by Buddhists or by Hindus. But the fact of our Lord's birth no one can safely ignore. Even Darrow had to date his legal papers, and that date is *anno domini*, "in the year of our Lord." Imagine the confusion that would result if each agnostic invented his or his own dating system.

Jesus Christ is a real person whose birth is a fact of history. The Communists taught their children that Jesus Christ never existed, that he was a myth invented by religious dictators in order to seduce and control people. But even the most liberal scholarship has not been able to erase Jesus Christ from history. More books have been written about Jesus Christ and his teachings than about any other subject. To ignore this fact is to close your mind to a whole area of truth that is just as valid as the latest space achievement or the newest discovery in medicine.

To ignore the coming of Jesus Christ into this world is
to rob yourself of the message of the Bible. If Jesus Christ
is a "humbug," then so is the Bible. He put his seal of
approval on the Old Testament Scriptures. His person and
work are the theme of the Gospels. His gospel is the message preached in the Book of the Acts. His doctrine is the
theme of the epistles, and his coming again is the subject
of the Book of the Revelation.

The person who ignores Jesus Christ can never really
understand human culture. My wife and I once leisurely
walked through a famous art museum where hundreds of
priceless paintings were exhibited, and I carefully noted
all of the masterpieces that in some way involved Jesus
Christ. I was amazed at their number.

Or, for that matter, consider the world of music. The
great classical composers wrote religious music that cen-
tered on either the person or the work of Jesus Christ. The
man or woman who refuses to consider Christ is really
refusing to enjoy and understand huge areas of human culture, and this is a tragedy.

Before I yielded my life for the gospel ministry, I wanted
to be a teacher; and (of all things) I wanted to teach literature and Latin. While my love for Latin has cooled, I am
still a reader of classic literature; and my knowledge of
Jesus Christ and the Bible makes my reading much more
meaningful. William Lyon Phelps, who headed the English department at Yale for many years, used to say that a
knowledge of the Bible apart from a college education is
more valuable than a college education without a knowledge of the Bible. He was right.

The person who chooses to ignore Jesus Christ is actually destroying himself; for Jesus Christ came as man to
show us what God wanted us to be. *He came as man that he
might die to make us what God wanted us to be.* The unbeliever
who ignores Jesus Christ leaves out of his life the only Per-

son who can save him from sin and then enable him to live a fulfilling life to the glory of God. Jesus said, "I have come that they may have life, and that they may have it more abundantly" (John 10:10).

In other words, the people who choose to ignore Jesus Christ are really practicing deception on themselves. They want all the good things of "Christian culture," but they do not want the Source of these good things. They have no problem enjoying a magnificent painting or a beautiful concert, but they will not acknowledge that Jesus Christ is important enough to know personally, to trust, and to follow. It is one thing to stand at the singing of Handel's "Hallelujah Chorus" and quite another thing to bow the knees and confess that Jesus Christ is Lord!

Why is it that these educated and seemingly intelligent people will practice this deception? Why will they accept the "Christ of culture" but not the Christ of history, the Christ of Calvary?

To begin with, there is an inborn bias in human nature that simply does not want God. "All we like sheep have gone astray: we have turned, every one, to his own way" (Isa. 53:6). Even the most brilliant scholar is born a lost sinner and has no innate desire to know God or to obey him. Jesus said, "I am . . . the truth" (John 14:6), but enslaved human nature refuses to face the truth and prefers to believe lies.

Evangelist Billy Sunday used to say that sinners cannot find God for the same reason criminals cannot find policemen: *They aren't looking!* The wise men who followed the star and knelt before the infant Christ were probably among the leading scholars of their day; yet they did not think it unscholarly to worship him. The light of nature (the star) led them to the light of the Word—"in Bethlehem of Judea, for thus it is written by the prophet" (Matt. 2:5); and both led them to the Christ child. These Oriental sci-

entists and philosophers had their limitations if we measure them by modern standards, but they are miles ahead
of modern scholars when it comes to facing facts honestly.

The person who ignores Jesus Christ does so at the peril
of his own soul. Christianity is an *exclusive* religion: "Neither is there salvation in any other," said Peter, "for there
is no other name under heaven given among men by which
we must be saved" (Acts 4:12). Our modern pluralistic society abhors this kind of exclusive message, tells Christians
they are narrow and arrogant, and argues that every religion is good if only the follower is sincere. People forget
that it's possible to be sincerely wrong.

God revealed the good news of the birth of Christ to
humble shepherds, not to pious priests or proud scholars.
The Jewish priests in Jerusalem could quickly find chap-
ter and verse to tell King Herod where the Messiah would
be born, but they themselves did nothing about it. And
they were only five miles from the Son of God.

It has always been the case that God hides his truth from
the wise and learned and reveals it to the childlike—shepherds, fishermen, little children, brokenhearted sinners. As
it was in Paul's day, so it is today: "Not many wise according to the flesh, not many mighty, not many noble, are
called. But God has chosen the foolish things of the world
to put to shame the wise" (1 Cor. 1:26–27). This does not
mean that God puts a premium on ignorance, but that the
wise in this world will not put a premium on the truth of
God. They know too much.

We need not defend everything that goes on in the celebration of the birth of Christ, because not everything is
motivated by a love for Christ or by faith in his Word. But
the fact of Christ's birth in Bethlehem cannot be ignored.
The man or woman who willfully ignores this momentous
event in history is making it clear that he or she has no
intentions of being honest. These people—educated or

uneducated—are deliberately blocking out of their thinking a whole area of truth that simply must not be ignored. If any scientist adopted that same approach in his laboratory experiments, he would be drummed out of the ranks as deceitful and dishonest.

I am not saying that a person must celebrate Christmas the way various people do. That is not important. What I am saying is that no person can afford to ignore the Christ whose birth is celebrated at Christmas. Jesus said, "For if you do not believe that I am He, you will die in your sins" (John 8:24).

Clarence Darrow was a brilliant lawyer but a terrible theologian. Expertise in one area is no guarantee of success in another. To advise people to pay no attention to Christmas is like telling a dying man to ignore the doctor, or a hungry man to ignore food on the table, or a wandering man to ignore the guide who came to lead him to safety. God invaded our planet; this is a fact of history. Nobody can safely ignore it.

18 CHURCH ON THE MOVE

I read recently that St. Paul's Cathedral in London is moving down Fleet Street at the rate of one inch every hundred years. When I mentioned this fact to a pastor friend, he replied, "Well, that's faster than most churches are moving!"

It does seem strange that the church should move so slowly in its ministry when God has shared with us his own dynamic power. When the Spirit of God came upon the early believers, they witnessed with such effectiveness that thousands trusted Christ. Before long, the powers that be were complaining that the disciples had "filled Jerusalem" with their message (Acts 5:28).

We should be moved, not only by God's power but also by our love for Him and for lost souls. Love is the greatest motive in the world. If we really love Christ, we should want to obey him. "If you love Me, keep My commandments" (John 14:15).

Never before in history has the church had greater opportunities or better tools to get the job done. I sometimes imagine what Paul might have accomplished if all the tools God has given to us—radio, television, jet planes, the printing press, and all the other miracles of modern science—had been available to him. I believe that these are God's gift to his people to help them accomplish his work in this present age. Are we using them effectively?

And while we are busy doing little, the cultists and the religious hucksters are working overtime to win and to brainwash converts. Sad to say, many of the people who join the cults used to attend conservative churches. They didn't find whatever they were looking for in the church, so they went shopping elsewhere.

We cannot stand still in the Christian life. We either go forward or gradually slide backward. This is also true of churches. Our churches ought to be marching armies, but too often they are comfortable museums. We believers ought to be witnesses, but instead we are prosecuting attorneys, arguing among ourselves. We are supposed to "proclaim the praises" of the God who has saved us (1 Pet. 2:9)—which literally means "to advertise God's wonderful character"—and yet we busy ourselves competing among ourselves and arguing over who is the greatest.

A church on the move must have leadership with vision and spiritual vitality. No "business as usual" meetings will do! The pastor simply cannot do it all, nor can he get the job done if the church leaders do not work with him. We need praying leaders, men and women with a concern for lost souls. We need to ask God to visit our meetings and do something different!

The prophet Isaiah had the same burden on his heart when he prayed, "Oh, that You would rend the heavens! That You would come down! That the mountains might shake at Your presence" (Isa. 64:1).

A church on the move must major on the Word of God, teaching and preaching the Word and (most of all) obeying it. We don't need elaborate programs, although there certainly ought to be planning and direction. What we need is the impact of God's Word through the lives of devoted people who love each other and love the lost. We pride ourselves on our expository preaching and our fine Bible-study literature, but is the Word of God accomplishing anything in our own lives? Are we "hearers" or "doers" of the Word (see James 1:22)?

Someone once asked me, "Why is it that church committees ask the wrong questions when they talk to pastoral candidates?" I asked him to elaborate, and he did. "Not one committee has asked me about my personal devotional life or my study habits or what my family life is like. All they ask about are routine things. Did I read the church constitution? Do I believe in personal visitation? How do I feel about Bible translations? I'm so discouraged about churches that I think I'll just start one of my own and try to make it different!"

Perhaps this is one answer to the question, "Why is the church progressing so slowly?" Some church leaders don't know what the spiritual priorities are. Sad to say, many church committees are just monitoring conformity, keeping the machinery going and trying to have as few problems as possible. But the absence of problems is often the evidence that nothing is happening. (There are few problems in a cemetery!)

There was plenty of friction in the early church. The spiritual leaders were arrested for their preaching. Hypocritical members dropped dead in the meeting. Deacons were stoned to death. There were even divisions in the church that had to be solved by love and prayer. The fact that our fellowship moves along smoothly may simply suggest that we are all too tired and powerless to raise much dust!

Spiritual pastors do not create problems; they reveal them. "Our new pastor has everybody on the board upset," a church officer confided in me. I knew something about the church and quietly gave thanks that God was working. Previous ministers had glossed over the real problems in the church and had kept everybody happy by rearranging the window dressing.

A church on the move is not afraid of change. Someone has said the "seven last words of the church" are "But we've always done it this way!" If I understand the Book of the Acts at all, I must admit that the early Christians were not afraid of change. They moved from city to city without complaining, carrying the gospel with them. They adjusted local church organization and ministry to their own situations. Like a mighty army, they advanced across the Roman Empire; they obeyed orders, accepted charges, maintained unity, and defeated the enemy.

A church on the move must confront reality and meet people where they are. Separation is not isolation—it is contact without contamination. Jesus was the friend of publicans and sinners. Many church members don't have any unsaved friends, or if they do, they keep them at a distance. Jesus was crucified outside Jerusalem, where the crowd was so cosmopolitan that the inscription on his cross had to be written in three languages. Many churches today have abandoned the marketplace and spend their time reminding one another of the gospel.

I believe in the local church. Even though I no longer pastor a local church, I have a pastor's heart and trust I always will. I love the church and have devoted my life to its ministry. I thank God for churches that are on the move, building up the saints, winning the lost, making an impact on their community and their world. I thank God for dedicated young men and women, graduating from our fine Christian schools, ready to sacrifice and serve in the church.

But I am concerned that our churches are not challenging these young people to do their best. Some of our best and brightest young men and women are lost to local church ministries because they don't want to spend their time doing what is routine. Many of these graduates want

to see something happen in the church, and they get discouraged when churches are satisfied with business as
usual. They want to light a fire for God, but somebody
keeps throwing water on it.

In the long run, this matter touches each of us personally. There is no such thing as churches doing anything;
whatever is done must be done by *individuals*. If you and
I are Christians on the move, then we will help to build
churches on the move.

How fast are we moving in our own spiritual lives?

19 LEARNING TO LISTEN

Three hundred years before Christ was born, the philosopher Zeno of Citium said, "The reason why we have two ears and only one mouth is that we may listen the more and talk the less." James had the same idea when he wrote: "Therefore, my beloved brethren, let every man be swift to hear, slow to speak, slow to wrath" (James 1:19).

Many people don't realize the importance of listening, as far as the Christian life is concerned. Often our Lord cried out, "Who has ears, let him hear!" The parable of the sower makes it clear that fruitfulness of life depends on faithfulness of listening.

I have concluded that we really don't know how to listen. There is something wrong with our whole approach to Bible lessons and Sunday sermons. For that reason, I want to make several suggestions—to myself as well as to you—that might help all of us get more out of the lesson or the sermon the next time we encounter the Word of God.

Preparation

What would you think of a pastor or Sunday-school teacher who came to church unprepared to preach or teach? Or perhaps the material was prepared, but the person was unprepared—weary, unenthusiastic, indifferent? You would probably conclude that the teacher or preacher was not taking spiritual responsibilities very seriously.

But how many times have you and I gone to God's house unprepared to hear his Word? We got little or nothing out of the message and returned home in worse spiritual condition than when we left—and we probably blamed it all on the pastor.

To begin with, we ought to prepare ourselves physically. The workers on the night shift may have to come to church weary, but there is no reason why most of us can't plan to arrive rested and at our best. A part of worship is presenting our bodies to God (see Rom. 12:1), and we should not give him that which is incapable of sincere worship. The Christian who goes to bed too late on Saturday night is going to rob himself and God on Sunday morning.

A weary body is usually the sign of a foggy mind. We must prepare our minds if we are going to listen to God's Word with any degree of understanding and enjoyment. I find that watching the news, reading the paper, or engaging in trifling conversation before worship all have a way of robbing my mind of the spiritual sensitivity I need to listen to God's Word. The believer who spends time each morning in the Word and prayer is the one who is best prepared to worship. The soil of the soul must be readied for the seed of the Word. James had this in mind when he wrote, "Therefore putting aside all filthiness and all that remains of wickedness, in humility receive the word implanted, which is able to save your souls" (James 1:21 NASB). We must pull out the weeds before we can receive the seeds.

If you have children in your home, then you must prepare the whole family. Nothing destroys our ability to enjoy the Word like arriving at church in the midst of a family feud. Junior couldn't find his shoes. Sister misplaced her Bible. Anybody who has raised children can add to this list *ad infinitum*.

When we parents are careless about our preparations for the Lord's Day, we are telling our children in a subtle way that going to Sunday school and church and hearing God's Word are not important matters to us. Father usually makes better preparations for his fishing trips than he does for Sunday services.

Take extra time on Saturday to get things together. Teach your children the importance of preparing to go to the house of God. Our attitude must not be that of an army preparing for battle, but of a group of God's people going to God's house to enjoy his Word.

Preparation is essential to good listening. Yes, it demands discipline, including saying no to many Saturday-night invitations; but the results are well worth the sacrifice.

Concentration

It requires concentration to listen and to learn. We must exercise our will and capture our thoughts and keep them under control. Human nature being what it is, we must expect to confront distractions and detours; but we must also yield our minds to the Lord and fight every effort of the enemy to confuse us.

You would think that the saints would encourage each other in this matter of concentration, but such is not always the case. Quite frankly, some of the biggest distractions in a worship service come from the saints—and not just the teenagers as they giggle and pass notes, because the adults can be equally distracting. Yet no matter what our situation, you and I must make every effort to focus our attention on the Word of God.

I find it helpful before the preaching begins to read the
Scripture passage under consideration. I don't try to
second-guess the pastor and anticipate his outline. Instead,
I allow God's Word to speak to my own heart as I read and
meditate. As the pastor speaks, I keep the Word before me
and notice what it says. I pray for him that the Spirit will
direct his words.

Concentration must be active, not passive. It is work!
But it is blessed work as we share in the excitement of hearing the Word of God.

"But our preacher is boring!" somebody argues. "It's
hard to concentrate when the preacher isn't saying anything."

Sad to say, some preachers are difficult to listen to, either
because they are poorly prepared or simply don't know
how to present the Word of God in an interesting manner.
Some men preach only because they have to say something, not because they really have something to say; and
that kind of preaching can be boring.

However, don't be too critical of the preacher, and don't
compare him Sunday by Sunday with your favorite media
minister. If your pastor is a dedicated man of God with a
burden to share God's truth, then concentrate on what he
says, and God will give you what you need. Outlook helps
to determine outcome. If your outlook is positive, not nega-
tive, then you will discover a blessing even in a message
you may think is boring.

Illumination

Often when I preach, I ask God to say far more to the
people than I say. God's message is not limited by the
preacher's outline. Many times the Lord has illumined his
Word for me in ways that the preacher in the pulpit never
expected. As I have listened to the Word, the Spirit has put
together truths he taught me the previous week; and the

result has been a better understanding of God's will for my life.

After all, real preaching is an act of worship, and listening to preaching ought to be an act of worship. We are not critics at a debate, spectators at an entertainment event, or passive pupils hearing a religious lecture. We are the people of God gathered to worship. We are not listening to get an outline or discover a new truth. We are there to worship God, to see him "high and lifted up." Preaching that obscures God is not biblical preaching, and listening that fails to bring us face to face with God is not true listening in the Spirit.

Illumination is the work of the Holy Spirit, and we must depend on him to teach us new truths and to remind us of truths we may have forgotten. When a congregation is "in the Spirit," the Word comes forth with power and penetration. We experience what the little girl in London meant when she said to her mother, "Mother, is Mr. Spurgeon speaking *to me*?" The Word becomes personal.

Too often we focus on the earthen vessel instead of looking at the treasure. Don't permit either the possible inexperience or incompetence of the preacher to rob you of the message God has for you. Ask God to say to your own heart far more than the preacher says with his lips, and he will bless you.

Application

The blessing doesn't come because we hear the Word; it comes because we do the Word. Anything else is pure deception.

Good feelings are not a substitute for obedience. "Wasn't that a great sermon!" says a worshiper. "I felt the Lord so near to me as he preached!" Fine, but the big test is not how I feel after church but how I act.

A parishioner said to her pastor, "You had a good sermon today until you got to all those *therefores*!" But the "therefores" are the reason why the sermon exists in the first place. God's Word is a light to guide us, and we must follow. It is water to wash us, and we must bathe. It is a mirror to show us our blemishes, and we must be honest. It is medicine to heal our hurts, and we must apply it. We don't just look at the Word or learn the Word; we must live by the Word (see Matt. 4:4).

Before we hear the Word, there must be preparation. As we hear the Word, there must be concentration and illumination. After we hear the Word, there must be application.

This is the only way to hear the Word of God and benefit from it.

"It was by the ear, by our first parents listening to the serpent, that we lost paradise," said the Puritan preacher Thomas Watson, "and it is by the ear, by hearing of the Word, that we get to heaven. 'Hear, and your soul shall live'" (Isa. 55:3).

After all, the fault may not lie with the preacher—it may lie with us, the listeners.

20 FORGIVEN—AND ENJOYING IT

*E*very honest Christian must admit that at times we disobey and disappoint God. To deny this fact would be to run against human experience and divine revelation. The great men and women we meet in the Bible all failed God at one time or another; only our wonderful Lord did not sin because in him there was no sin.

Therefore, it is a good thing to know that God forgives the sins of his own children. We all know the promise so well: "If we confess our sins, He is faithful and just to forgive us our sins, and to cleanse us from all unrighteousness" (1 John 1:9). How many times we have reminded God of his promise. And how many times he has been faithful to keep it.

Once we have confessed our sin and claimed his promise, we know that we are forgiven. But often, we do not experience forgiveness within. Not that we demand some kind of emotional earthquake; but there are times when we would like to have an inner assurance from the Father that all is well. To be sure, feelings can be treacherous. It is possible to feel forgiven and not really be forgiven at all. On the other hand, it is possible to have forgiveness from the Father and yet feel as though we are still far from the Father's house and heart.

Is there anything we can do to experience forgiveness after we have received forgiveness? Yes, there are several steps we can take that can result in a deeper experience of God's forgiveness.

First and most important is to *turn immediately to the Word*. When a husband and wife are at odds with each other, they stop communicating. Silence reigns in the home. But when there is forgiveness, hearts and lips are opened again, and words go to work, tearing down walls and building bridges.

God wants to talk to you, and he does it through his Word. After you have been restored to fellowship, turn to God's Word and spend time meditating on it. Old truths will take on new meaning, and new truths will jump out at you from familiar verses. The Word will come like medicine to your broken heart, and you will experience a joy within as you realize that your Father is speaking to you again.

If when you read the Word, God is silent, then I suggest you humbly examine your own heart to see if your confession of sin was full and sincere. Are you hiding anything? Are you bargaining with God? Was there true repentance or just regret because you got caught? The very Word that is silent to us can also penetrate our hearts and expose our thoughts and motives. David knew that God desired truth "in the inward parts" (Ps. 51:6), so he did not stop with a mere surface confession.

A second step is this: *Do everything possible to make things right with others*. Often there is a spiritual decline in our lives before we sin, and during that time we could easily hurt the people we live with or work with. After we sin and get out of fellowship with God, we can do terrible damage to others. If our confession has been sincere, we will want to do everything possible to correct these things and make matters right with others.

I had not been preaching very long in my first church when I realized a coldness in my heart and a barrenness in my ministry. God showed me that I owed an apology to a pastor I had wronged. It was not easy to phone him for an appointment, go to his home, and there apologize for what I had said and done; but I did it. Once that matter was settled, God filled my heart anew with his presence and began to bless my ministry. I had confessed my sin privately to the Lord, and he had forgiven me; but the experience of forgiveness did not come until I had made things right with a brother.

Now, some people carry this too far and make nuisances of themselves. I recall one church member who used to ask me to forgive her for things she had thought about me. As long as the sin is between you and the Lord, don't make it public. It is when we have openly sinned against another believer that we have to deal with it openly and personally. In fact, the wider the consequences, the wider must be the confession. There is no need to have perpetual spiritual autopsies just to find something to confess.

Some years ago, I conducted a brief Bible conference at a church whose pastor had resigned the day before the conference opened. There was a great deal of ill will in the congregation because of his departure; you could feel it in the public services. But the Lord used the Word to break through one evening, and people actually ran across the church auditorium to seek forgiveness and to pray together. It was a high and holy hour, and it opened the floodgates of blessing.

"Well, I've confessed it to the Lord," we argue, "so I don't have to apologize to anybody else." That kind of an attitude may be evidence that we have not really confessed our sins to God. A broken heart toward God cannot be a hard heart toward men. If I have honestly humbled myself before the Father, I should have no problem humbling myself before one of his children.

I have a feeling that the Spirit is grieved more by our proud attitude of self-righteousness than perhaps by any other sin that we Christians commit. And yet, if we want to experience forgiveness in our hearts, we must be certain there is nothing between us and our brothers and sisters in Christ.

Let me suggest a third step: *Don't look back*. Satan will do all that he can to remind you of your sins. After all, he is the "accuser of the brethren"—and he might even use some of the brethren to remind you. It is impossible to wipe out the memory of past acts; even Paul recalled that he had been a blasphemer and a murderer. But we must be careful that we respond in a spiritual way to the memory of past sins.

If we recall that sin with excitement and enjoyment, then we have not really judged it and confessed it. But if the memory of that sin brings to our hearts and minds a holy revulsion, then we are moving in the right direction.

If we say to ourselves, "How could I have done such a thing?" then we have not really faced our sins in humility and honesty. After all, we are capable of committing any sin! The ability is always there, but the desire must never be cultivated. To convince ourselves that what we did was really an exception, is only to set ourselves up for the next temptation. "Let him who thinks he stands take heed lest he fall" (1 Cor. 10:12).

The memory of past sin ought to drive us to our knees in prayer and dedication. It ought to make us hate sin more and love Jesus Christ in a deeper way. Whenever the devil reminds you of your sin, look immediately to Jesus Christ. When Satan talks to us about Jesus, he always lies; but when he talks to us about ourselves, he often tells the truth.

Look to Jesus Christ for cleansing, for assurance, for love, for all that you need.

Let me suggest another step: *Forgive others.* Our Lord's parable of the unforgiving servant (Matt. 18:21–35) makes it clear that there is a difference between receiving forgiveness and sharing forgiveness. One of the marks of a truly forgiven person is his willingness to forgive others. We first have to forgive them in our hearts before we share forgiveness in our actions and words. I cannot harbor malice toward my brother and expect God to forgive me. We need to meditate on Ephesians 4:32 and Colossians 3:13.

Finally, let me suggest the step of *service.* This does not mean that we earn God's forgiveness; forgiveness can come only through the work of Christ on the cross. The prodigal son wanted to work his way back into his father's fellowship, but the father would not permit it. However, the fact that the boy was willing to become a lowly servant was evidence to the father that his son had truly repented. If you want to experience a deeper peace and joy in your heart after you have gotten right with God, ask him to use you to minister to somebody else. "Freely you have received, freely give" (Matt. 10:8).

We who defend the truth of the Bible are often guilty of having truths in our mind but not experiences in our heart. We know we are forgiven "because the Bible tells us so." But the Father wants us to have more than "paper forgiveness." He wants to do something wonderful in our hearts. He wants forgiveness to be an experience, not just an event. After all, when two estranged people forgive each other and restore their fellowship, it is more than a cut-and-dried formal event. There may well be tears, laughter, a new freedom in conversation, all of which are evidences that something internal has taken place.

God can do something in us as well as for us as he forgives and cleanses us. In this way, he helps us to hate sin more and love him more. This fortifies us against the future assaults of the enemy. It also edifies us and helps us in helping others who have sinned. True forgiveness leads to fellowship, and fellowship leads to service. Forgiveness is not probation; it is restoration—and that should lead to rejoicing!

21 WHAT'S IN IT FOR ME?

*D*iagnosticians of society and its ills like to give names to each period and generation. We have had the Aspirin Age and the Beat Generation. You may remember the Lost Generation and the Now Generation. I seem to recall that the Nervous Generation was functioning in the early 1960s. The experts tell us that a new kind of society is now here—the Me Generation.

To put it bluntly, the Me Generation is selfish and thinks only of its own interests and pleasures. The noted Harvard sociologist David Riesman called it "egocentrism," which is just a highbrow word for selfishness. The slogan of this new society is "Do your own thing, and do it your own way." Their goal in life is to take care of themselves.

There is nothing new under the sun. This Me Generation has been with us ever since Eve decided to do her own thing and Adam decided to follow her example. Human nature is basically sinful, which means that it is basically selfish. Babies are born selfish, but this selfishness is a means for staying alive. The tragedy is that many people do not grow out of that infantile selfishness, and society seems to encourage them.

You would think that the new birth—that spiritual and moral revolution that accompanies faith in Jesus Christ—would do away with selfishness; but the cure is not immediate or complete. Unfortunately, most of us are still "prone to wander" and like lost sheep, we still want to turn "every one to his own way." The malady shows itself in the church member who abandons his church because he is not getting anything out of it. It shows itself in that husband or wife who says, "I'm not getting anything out of this marriage" and takes off.

Where in the Bible are we told that we are supposed to get something out of church? Somebody has said that the local church is like the neighborhood bank—you get nothing out of it until you put something into it. And as for marriage, who ever said that its main purpose was to please either the husband or the wife? Scripture passages like Ephesians 5:22–33 and 1 Corinthians 7:1–5 seem to indicate that mutual marital enrichment depends on something far deeper than mere enjoyment. "I'm not getting anything out of my marriage!" may be a confession that someone is not putting anything into the marriage.

Christians cannot afford to belong to the Me Generation because Christians belong to the body of Christ. This means that we belong to each other. It also means that we have the privilege and responsibility of ministering to one another. I have counted at least fourteen places in the New Testament where we are told to "love one another." I have noticed more than twenty other references in the New Testament that use the words *one another,* such as "edify one another," "admonish one another," "bear one another's burdens," "care for one another," and so on. People who take these commandments seriously will have a hard time belonging to the Me Generation.

No doubt one cause for this "Christian egocentrism" is the emphasis we have been placing on personal Christianity. The individual is the important thing, not the family or the church. A large proportion of books marketed to believers today emphasizes the individual experience almost to the denial of the importance of the local assembly. Much of our newer music centers on personal testimony—"what Jesus did for *me*"—without ever relating that experience to the needs of the whole family of God or of a lost world. Some of the worst culprits are the sincere, well-meaning saints who conduct various seminars that seek to build up the individual instead of helping the individual build the church.

We are emerging from an era of superstars and celebrities, people who have used Christians to build up their ministries instead of using their ministries to build up Christians. In our reaction to this change, we may find ourselves drifting into "evangelical egocentrism" without realizing it. Like Peter, we may find ourselves asking, "Lord, what shall we get?" (see Matt. 19:27). With the Lord's help, like Peter we can change that statement to "Such as I have give I thee" (Acts 3:6). After all, it is not a great step from "What will I get?" to "What can I give?"—provided you take that step at Calvary.

The cross of Jesus Christ exposes the hollowness of the Me Generation and its philosophy. It is one thing for us to sing "In the Cross of Christ I Glory" and quite something else for us to lay down our lives for the brethren. The cross and selfishness cannot cooperate; they must constantly be in conflict. "And those who are Christ's have crucified the flesh with its passions and desires" (Gal. 5:24). That should take care of our selfishness!

I fear that the Me Generation philosophy will penetrate the church more and more in the days to come. It is something we must oppose with every spiritual weapon at our disposal. We must pray, "Not my will, but thy will be done." We must look upon our local church, not as a fellowship for entertainment where we get something out of it, but as a fellowship for investment and employment where we put something into it. Individual Christianity is important, but it must not remain individual. The Lord's Prayer does not begin with "My Father," but "Our Father." Even when we pray, we cannot ignore one another.

I have a feeling that the saints who think of others are the ones who, in the long run, will get the most out of it. No matter what the modern faddists are saying, it is still the person who loses his life for the sake of others who finds it. The most satisfying life has always been the most sacrificial life, and this applies in the home as well as in the church. When you put yourself into it, you receive dividends now—and forever!

22 WANTED: DISCERNING CHRISTIANS

*I*f you want to escape a great deal of trouble and misunderstanding in your life, learn to distinguish between conviction, opinion, prejudice, and taste. It has well been said that an opinion is something that you hold, but a conviction is something that holds you. Most of us have very few convictions, but the ones we do have are important to us. Convictions are the compasses of life—they keep us moving in the right direction. They are the foundation stones that help us to stand firm when everything around us is shaking and changing.

There are usually no convictions without convulsions. You can pick up new opinions at a coffee break, but true convictions come out of real conflict and suffering. Just as Isaac had to dig again the wells that his father dug (see Gen. 26:17–33), so each new generation has to discover for itself the power and reality of spiritual convictions. A secondhand faith is not faith at all.

There is a well-known story told about George Whitefield, the evangelist. He asked a man what he believed, and the man replied, "I believe what my church believes."

"What does your church believe?" Whitefield asked.

"My church believes what I believe," was the answer.

"Well, what do you *both* believe?" asked the evangelist.

"We both believe the same thing!"

That man thought he had convictions, but all he really had were secondhand opinions.

The doctrinal and ethical convictions of the Christian faith are not complicated, and most, if not all, evangelical believers would endorse them and, if necessary, die for them. These convictions about God, Jesus Christ, the Holy Spirit, the Bible, and God's plan for fallen man have motivated and directed the church for centuries. These doctrinal and ethical norms have been attacked in the past and are being attacked today, but God's eternal truth will stand and withstand all the onslaughts of the enemy.

We get our convictions with difficulty, but opinions are easy to obtain and easy to change. There is no explaining why we hold the opinions that we do. Some opinions are carefully thought out and are readily defended, but no opinion should grip us the way a true conviction should hold us. Opinions may be debatable, but convictions are not. We may certainly discuss our convictions and dig deeper into the basic principles of the faith, but we do not debate whether these principles are true or false.

Opinions grow out of the varied experiences of life. After flying thousands of miles on various airlines, I have the opinion that certain airlines are better than others; but I cannot prove my opinion with statistics or scientific data. I have ministered the Word in many Bible conferences, and I have opinions about them; but only God knows the truth about them. My opinions have a way of changing as I mature in life, and perhaps yours do too.

It is dangerous to treat a shallow opinion with the same respect that we give to a settled conviction. As Christians, we must learn to accept each other's opinions and not make them a test of spirituality or fellowship.

Ambrose Bierce defined prejudice as "a vagrant opinion without visible means of support." Prejudice is often a child of ignorance, and it can be stubborn and unmoving. We can defend our convictions from the Word of God, and we can even explain our opinions from our own experiences in life; but prejudice is something we refuse to examine honestly—probably because we are afraid we might be proved wrong. We all have our prejudices, some of which we inherited from the atmosphere of our home or school, while others we have picked up like excess baggage along the way. I suppose it may not do a great deal of damage to have prejudices, as long as we recognize them and don't allow them to control our lives.

Some prejudices, of course, are sheer poison. To claim that one race is superior to another or that handicapped people should be treated as second-class citizens is dangerous nonsense.

Prejudice is often the result of taste, and there is no way to explain taste. I prefer classical music, somebody else prefers "easy listening" music, and some people don't like music at all. I enjoy eating Chinese food, but some of my friends will never touch it. (Have you ever had a friend order spaghetti in a Chinese restaurant?)

I think that we Christians agree on what God wants us to do: worship him, grow in grace, love and serve others, and take the gospel to a lost world. But we don't always agree on how these things are supposed to be accomplished. We agree on the ends because of our convictions, but we don't always agree on the means to the ends. When it comes to applying our convictions, our opinions and prejudices have a way of asserting themselves—and sometimes we don't know the difference between them.

Take the matter of calling a pastor. No evangelical church would even consider a candidate who denied the virgin birth or the work of Christ on the cross. Our convictions tell us that. But where do we go from there? The younger people in the church want a younger pastor, while the older people want a "more mature man" who will understand their problems. One deacon wants an expositor who teaches the Bible a verse at a time, while another deacon wants a preacher who encourages and inspires him with life-centered sermons. I have even met church officers who have opposed a new pastor because he reminded them of former pastors they didn't like.

Consider the area of church music. Centuries ago, it was a policy that only David's psalms could be used in public worship. (They overlooked Ephesians 5:19: "psalms and hymns and spiritual songs.") When gifted men and women began to produce newer songs—still based on Scripture—they were severely criticized. When churches began to introduce instrumental music into the services, some of the saints were sure God's judgment would fall. (They should hear what goes on in some churches today!) Even Moody and Sankey ran into brick walls of prejudice when they ministered in Britain, because Sankey used a portable organ and sang songs other than the psalms.

We seem to forget that the great hymns of the faith were at one time new songs, and that many of them were attacked and criticized.

When we act on the basis of real conviction, we are not afraid of the truth. We know that all truth is God's truth and that all truth intersects. But when we are acting on the basis of prejudice or opinion, we usually will not face facts or discuss the matter in depth. "My mind is made up—don't confuse me with facts!" This explains why prejudiced people never learn anything new: They already know everything! These are the people who write hateful letters that say, "Cancel my subscription" or who march out of a church service because the pastor read a verse from a different translation of the Bible.

I was once criticized by a student who disapproved of some of the books I have written because in them I quoted from different translations. "The King James Version is the *only* Bible," he told me. "It's the only *authorized* Word of God!"

When he had calmed down, I asked him to answer three questions for me: What was the Word of God before 1611 when the King James Version was published? What is the Word of God on the mission fields where people cannot read English? Who authorized the King James Version to be the Word of God?

Of course, he saw the plight he was in. If some person or group authorized a translation to be the Word of God, then that person or group would have a higher authority than the Bible itself. And it is inconceivable that the great saints and martyrs from Pentecost to 1611 did not have the Word of God. It is even more inconceivable that our missionaries, who dedicate their lives to the translation and distribution of the Bible, are wasting their time on publications that are not the Word of God.

My student friend's prejudices were showing, but when I confronted him with truth, he refused to budge. I can only pray for him and ask God to open his eyes.

The next time you and I find ourselves in disagreement, let's stop to ask, "Is this a matter of conviction, opinion, prejudice, or taste?" If it is a matter of conviction, then we ought to be able to go to the Bible and to the throne of grace and get the matter settled. We need to love each other and be patient with each other. But my feeling is that few disagreements stem from differences about convictions. Most of our disunity grows out of personal opinions and prejudices.

There is room for variety and diversity in the church. Our Lord's twelve apostles were not all alike. Some prejudices are dead wrong while others are harmless and even comical. Our opinions change from year to year and sometimes from week to week. It is possible for saints to disagree without disturbing the unity of the church, and God can bless people we disagree with!

May the Lord give us discernment to know who our enemy really is and what battles are really worth fighting.

23 THE FILE-CARD MENTALITY

*Y*ears ago, A. W. Tozer used to warn us about what he called "the file-card mentality." This is the mindset that categorizes everything, has a pigeonhole in which to put everything, and rarely if ever makes any changes in the file.

Of course, some things that we pigeonhole will never change. Sin is sin, and it must always be filed as sin. Obedience is obedience, and truth is truth. I am not suggesting that Christians be so open-minded that every wind of doctrine can blow right through their heads! Once we have settled a matter with the Lord, it is finished business and need not be put on the agenda again.

However, evangelical Christians do tend to cultivate the file-card mentality whether they realize it or not. For example, we can have this attitude when we read the Bible: This book is for the Jews, this one for the church, and this one for somebody else. Now, I understand enough about serious Bible study to know that we must follow logical principles of interpretation; otherwise, we will end up making the Bible say things it was never meant to say. Almost every cult claims biblical authority for its false doctrines, simply because cult leaders practice subtle forms of misinterpretation.

What I am warning against is the mindset that so pigeonholes the various parts of Scripture that the Book loses its power. The Bible is like our Lord's seamless robe and we must be careful not to tear it to pieces. Of course, none of the Bible was written to us (because we were born too late), but all of the Bible was written for us. And all of the Bible is profitable if we will let the Holy Spirit enlighten us and enable us.

Practicing the file-card mentality is one of the best ways to avoid spiritual responsibility. If a portion of Scripture really convicts you, read it again, and see if you can't put it in somebody else's mailbox. King David did that when Nathan told him the story about the little ewe lamb (see 2 Sam. 12). David put a death notice in the rich man's mailbox. But then Nathan readdressed it, and sent it to David: "You are the man" (v. 7). I give David credit that he accepted the announcement and didn't try to send it to the dead-letter office.

The word *hermeneutics* may be a new one to you. It simply means "the science of interpretation," and it deals especially with the interpretation of the Bible. In recent months, I have been reading a great deal in the field of hermeneutics, and I am disturbed by one fact: many writers are so locked into their system that they leave no room for the Spirit to speak. Everything is cut and dried. I understand their principles, and I applaud their purpose; but I am disturbed by their mechanical treatment of the living Word of God. The wind of the Spirit is not permitted to blow wherever he wills; he must obey their rules.

Perhaps this explains why too many sermons are outlines and not nourishing spiritual meals. I am not against outlines, for I use them myself in my preaching and writing; but an outline is not a sermon any more than a recipe is a meal or a blueprint is a building. We fill our notebooks and inflate our heads, but our hearts are still cold and empty. We grow in knowledge without growing in grace. Blessed is that pastor or Sunday-school teacher who not only sets an orderly table but also puts some good food on the plates!

We can also develop the file-card mentality when it comes to people and ministries. It is so easy to put labels on people and think we are really identifying them. I realize that we need labels on certain products to warn people about danger, and some religious leaders and organizations need to be labeled *dangerous*. But we must take care that we don't start inventing labels that God never meant us to use. The New Testament tells us about those who uphold the faith and those who deny it; and these two categories have stood the test of time. Why add to them?

The issue is not between the orthodox and the liberal, because those lines are pretty clearly drawn. The problem comes when we try to pigeonhole the various kinds of orthodox people in the church today. In my personal research into the lives of great preachers, I have been repeatedly amazed at how difficult it is to categorize some of God's spiritual giants. For example, I have been greatly helped by the books written by Bishop J. C. Ryle (1816–1900). For twenty years he served as the Bishop of Liverpool and was faithful to the Word, yet some in the Anglican Church called him a compromiser. In fact, he was probably the first man in church history to be called a neo-evangelical. Where do we put him in our file?

Now, the problem with labels is that the people who make them (including ourselves) may not be competent judges, or they may judge on the basis of faulty or incomplete facts. One person makes his evaluation on the basis of what translation a preacher uses; another looks at his library; a third investigates his friends; and still another asks him what school he attended. Very few pause to apply the greatest test of all: "By their fruits ye shall know them" (Matt. 7:20). What is the result of their life and ministry? Are people blessed and helped? Are they drawn closer to Christ? Is Jesus Christ glorified in their ministry?

It came as a hard lesson for me to learn, but I have discovered that God can bless people I disagree with. I am not talking about those who deny our Lord, but about born-again people who may have different ideas and interpretations, or different methods, from my own.

A third area where the file-card mentality is damaging is in the matter of God's will. Many people think that God's will is so rigid that their every mistake destroys some vast eternal plan and renders them helpless to serve God.

Most of the decisions you and I make each day are based on common sense. If we are in fellowship with God and commit ourselves to him, then he will guide us. If we start to go astray, he will check us. If we disobey and fail to judge and confess that sin, he will chasten us. But we must never think that our failings are too great for either God's grace or his power.

There is among some believers an almost neurotic preoccupation with the will of God. They are so busy with rules and formulas for discerning God's will that they have little time to fellowship with the God whose will they pretend to want more than anything else. How foolish! The best way to know God's mind is to get close to his heart and obey what he has already commanded. We must not be like the centipede who ran swiftly until the ant asked him how he knew which leg to move next. The poor centipede became so confused that he couldn't run at all!

There is nothing sinful in making plans, keeping goals before us, and seeking to make the best use of our time. But I fear that we sometimes so pigeonhole the will of God that we leave no room for his delightful interruptions and surprises. In trying to manage our time, we mangle our opportunities, and we miss those "inspired interruptions" that so delight the heart of God. The file-card mentality makes sure that everything is on schedule—and that everything is painfully dull.

If anybody in the Bible had a file-card mentality it was the apostle Peter, until the Lord matured him. Peter's filing system informed him that Jesus was not to die on the cross. It also informed him that he was to protect Jesus with the sword when the soldiers invaded Gethsemane. When God gave Peter the thrilling opportunity of taking the gospel to the Gentiles (see Acts 10), Peter's filing system had a ready answer: "Not so, Lord, for I have never—!" What Peter would have missed if God had limited himself to Peter's file-card approach to the Christian life!

Yes, there is security in the file-card mentality, but there is also rigidity and the awful potential for immaturity. One of my seminary professors used to remind us, "God is infinitely original!"

Perhaps we would have fewer carbon-copy Christians and churches if we really believed that!

24 SPEAKING OF SPIRITUAL THINGS

*A*mong the meaningful quotations that I have under the glass on my desk, the one from Bishop B. F. Westcott, the New Testament scholar, often arrests my attention. It says: "Every year makes me tremble at the daring with which people speak of spiritual things."

The way a person discusses spiritual matters is often an indication of the condition of his heart. People who have a close walk with God do not jest about the things of God, nor do they speak of them in a casual offhanded manner. Shallow Christians converse about God, the Bible, worship, and the cross as though they were talking about the weather or the latest fashions.

I am not suggesting, of course, that we adopt a solemn attitude and a holy tone of voice when we talk about the things of God. Stuffy piety can be as bad as the casual familiarity that lies at the other extreme. I am suggesting that we take care lest we cheapen the riches of our Christian faith by speaking of them with too much familiarity. Words, like coins, tend to lose their sharp image when they are handled too much.

For example, Christians giving a public testimony need to guard against this danger. Nothing kills the spirit of a meeting like the religious speechmakers who go on and on in their "testimony," talking more about themselves than the Lord. And when they do mention the Lord, their words are so daringly familiar that you would think they had just returned from a trip to the third heaven. Discerning saints who listen sense that the believers who gave the "testimony" had put more into the talk than the walk. How easy it is to run ahead of our experience, and the whole thing becomes sounding brass and a tinkling cymbal.

But we who minister God's Word must take heed as well. How easy it is to give people the impression that we know it all and have lived it all. We need to minister to ourselves before we minister to others. It is so easy to sound religious on paper or in a pulpit. It is quite something else to practice what we preach in our daily lives.

While I am on the subject, let me apply this to Christian singers. Music is a gift from God, and it has power to influence people in ways that the mere spoken word cannot. No singer has the right to sing a lie any more than a preacher has the right to preach a lie. In one of my pastorates, we had a young lady with a beautiful voice who often sang solos. Unfortunately, she was rather careless in her personal life, and she became engaged to an unsaved man. One Sunday, I learned that she was going to sing "Submission," a truly beautiful song; but I put a stop to it. I had refused to perform the marriage ceremony, and I certainly was not going to let her "perform" in church when she was openly defying God's standards for Christian marriage.

Another person comes to mind when I think of the seriousness of speech: Christians who tell jokes about the Bible. I will not repeat any of these so-called jokes lest I infect some innocent mind; but most of us have heard them. The Bible is not a joke book, even though it contains humor. Nobody appreciates true humor more than I do, but I fail to find anything laughable in these "Bible jokes." Such feeble attempts to be funny cheapen the inspired Word of God and tell everybody around that such jokesters do not take the Bible too seriously. I have even heard preachers tell "Bible jokes" from the pulpit. No unsaved person present would take his sermon seriously, you can be sure.

We expect unsaved people to speak carelessly about spiritual things because they have no spiritual life themselves. When they call God "The Man Upstairs," we cringe inwardly, but we understand that they simply don't know any better. The actress who called Jesus "a Livin' Doll" is to be pitied more than censured, because our wonderful Lord is a stranger to her. But when we hear professed believers use this kind of Hollywood jargon, we have reason to be concerned.

Now, before I am grossly misunderstood by some sincere reader, let me quickly add: I am not advocating that we all start speaking in King James English, as do some of our Quaker friends. The issue is not vocabulary or diction, but reality and truth. Solomon had this in mind when he wrote: "Be not rash with thy mouth, and let not thine heart be hasty to utter any thing before God" (Eccles. 5:2). Jesus echoed this truth when he said: "But let your communication be, Yea, yea; Nay, nay: for whatsoever is more than these cometh of evil" (Matt. 5:37).

The person of Christian character, whose walk with God reveals itself in practical ways, does not have to do a great deal of speaking to convince us that he knows God. It has been my experience that true men and women of God are "swift to hear, slow to speak" (James 1:19). In conducting business meetings in the Lord's work, I have often noticed how immature Christians like to make speeches and monopolize the agenda, while the seasoned saints hold their peace and speak only when the Spirit prompts them.

A few words from the latter group carries much more weight than all the speeches of the former group.

Our orthodox Jewish friends refuse to allow the name of God to pass their lips. While I disagree with the practice, I applaud the reverence that it shows for the Lord. Like any other practice, it can degenerate into an empty tradition; but the sentiment behind the practice is still a good one. Too often, we Christians use the name of the Lord in a flippant, overly-familiar way. Sometimes we do it in our praying.

In his own high-priestly prayer (recorded in John 17), the Savior was content to address the Father simply as "Father," or "righteous Father" or "holy Father." We have improved on this and address the Father using all kinds of elaborate adjectives, none of which I will mention lest I encourage the practice. Again, we may be sincere in such praying; but I wonder if perhaps we may unconsciously be trying to impress people with our "deep spirituality."

Anyone who has raised a family knows that most children go through a talking stage when life is filled with words. Some teens repeat that stage. They have the mistaken notion that if they talk about something, they have really done it. (People like this often find their way onto committees!) They make great speeches, but the words never change their lives. They are sincere, and if you challenged them, they would be shocked; but the results are always the same: all talk, no action. "Cheap talk" is what the world calls it. Solomon expressed it with a bit more force: "A fool vents all his feelings" (Prov. 29:11).

The world is not impressed with the excess of religious verbiage that we Christians tend to manufacture. They hear words all day long, advertising, propaganda, promotion; and they turn it off. Better that we should utter a few choice words, backed up by a sincere heart, than that we should smother people with words and turn them away from the gospel. And far better that we should say nothing than that we should speak lightly or carelessly about the precious things of the Christian life.

We do not have to curse or swear to take God's name in vain. All we have to do is use his name in some trivial manner and we have blasphemed. Undue familiarity can cheapen the divine name as much as open blasphemy. Speaking about precious spiritual matters in a common, trite way is sin just as much as denying these truths. We all have our collection of religious cliches, those counterfeit coins that pass for the real thing; and we all cheapen our witness by using them.

What is the remedy? I think it begins when we ask God to cleanse our hearts and forgive us for verbal hypocrisy. It continues as we seek reality in our spiritual lives, and as we live to please God and not to impress people. It grows as we refuse to allow vain words to clutter up our minds and hearts and as we seek to express ourselves simply and honestly. As we grow in our reverence for God, we cannot help but express this experience as we speak.

The prayer of the psalmist is what we need: "Let the words of my mouth and the meditation of my heart be acceptable in Your sight, O LORD, my strength and my redeemer" (Ps. 19:14).

25   REMEDY FOR BELIEVER'S BURNOUT

*I*f there is one word that best describes the average pastor or church member today, it is the word *busy*. Schedules are full, days are hectic, demands are getting greater and greater. The mark of the successful Christian these days seems to be a full calendar, a weary mind and body, and a lonely family. Without realizing it, we have adopted the pace and standard of the world, and somehow we expect to escape the price that the world is paying—fractured marriages, nervous breakdowns, emotional burnout, and various degrees of depression and inability to cope.

There is certainly nothing wrong with sincere ambition and the desire to build God's work. But we must take care that our standards of success are God's standards and not those of Madison Avenue or Hollywood. The American obsession with size and statistics has, I fear, captured us to the point of driving us toward goals that may or may not be biblical. This I do know: we are in danger of losing far more than we gain if we remain on this evangelical treadmill.

One cannot help but be impressed with our Lord's ministry when he was on earth. We never find him rushing about to get things done; nor do we hear him lament, "If I only had more time!" The reason? He lived in the Father's will and sought only to please the Father's heart. "Are there not twelve hours in the day?" he asked his disciples (John 11:9); and the apostle John in his Gospel keeps reminding us that Jesus was on a divine timetable and his hour had not yet come (see 2:4).

I was complaining one day to a friend that I had too much to do and simply could not take time for another meeting. He smiled and quietly said, "There is always time for the will of God." He hit the nail on the head: not everything in my datebook was in the will of God. I was so anxious to get things done and to please a lot of people that I was becoming the victim of my own ministry.

Jesus took time to get away from the crowd and rest his body and refresh his soul. He started his day in prayer and derived from that fellowship the strength he needed for the demands of the day. He was constantly in communion with the Father so that his decisions were in the will of God. He walked through each day with a holy calmness that radiated confidence, love, patience, and power. No wonder he could say, "Come to Me, . . . and I will give you rest" (Matt. 11:28).

It was while Peter "tarried many days in Joppa" that God opened the heavens and revealed the next stage of the gospel witness (Acts 9:43 KJV). According to some zealous preachers I have heard, Peter should have been out preaching to the needy multitudes.

I don't doubt that Peter had a ministry in Joppa after he raised Dorcas from the dead, but we get the impression that he was also taking time to think, meditate, and pray. Every Christian needs to experience "tarrying times" when he slows down long enough for God to catch up with him and perhaps teach him some new truths.

For some reason, we have the idea that tarrying times are idle times, and that Satan is just waiting to pounce on us when we sit still too long. To be sure, we can get into trouble if we tarry for the purpose of avoiding responsibility or of selfishly pleasing our own hearts. It was while David "tarried in Jerusalem" that he saw Bathsheba and sinned greatly; but I suspect that he had seen her before and had tarried for the purpose of taking her. As Vance Havner said, "David was making arrangements to sin."

No, our tarrying times must not be idle times. They must be quiet times when we devote ourselves to the Word of God and to prayer. They must be times when we get away from the routine and pause long enough for spiritual rest and recuperation. According to the Bible, waiting before God does not mean doing nothing. Rather, it means devoting all our attention and energy to God as we tarry before him.

In my travels, I have met pastors, missionaries, and church leaders who are about to burn out because they have exhausted their physical and spiritual energy. One of the best things a church member could do would be to babysit with the pastor's children so the pastor and his wife could get away and tarry before God. Church leaders who work hard all day, and then devote their evenings to the church, need to get away with their families and let God do some new thing for them. In our zeal to build the church, we may find ourselves tearing down the home.

Like you, I often find it difficult to say no. But we have to do it. If we don't build margins into our lives, we will soon find ourselves boxed in, and that box might become a coffin. We need breathing space. We need to forget the timetable occasionally and just *live*. The violinist knows that he must not keep his bow taut, so he loosens it after each performance. Is it any wonder we produce discord when our lives are stretched day after day to the breaking point?

We Christians pride ourselves on not being worldly. We shun alcohol, tobacco, and impure entertainment; but at the same time we join the world's rat race and compete with each other for all the time we can get. We forget that God gives each of us only twenty-four hours a day. The entire universe operates a day at a time while we attempt to cram a week's work into a weekend.

In the final analysis, it still takes time to be holy. The great masters of the spiritual life in church history were not jet-propelled. They were not afraid to be alone, to wait. When I was in high school, I had to read John Milton's "Sonnet on His Blindness"; and for the life of me, I could not understand the meaning of the last line: "They also serve who only stand and wait." Today, I have a better grasp of what the blind English poet was trying to say, even though I may not always practice it.

Perhaps the thrust of my message is simply this: all of us who seek to serve God must have tarrying days if we are to be effective. Otherwise, our ministry will become only activity—and feverish activity at that—and it will tear us down instead of build us up. We cannot solve everybody's problems. We cannot answer everybody's questions. We cannot accept everybody's invitations. We cannot participate in all the good works pleading for our help. Each of us must find the Father's will and live by that schedule.

Having said that, let me add: times of tarrying are preparation for times of toiling. We wait before the Lord so that we can work for the Lord. God is our refuge in the hiding place that he might be our strength in the marketplace. We go apart to be with him, not to escape life, but to get new enduement to face life. Tarrying times are times of refreshment and renewal. They are times of honest evaluation, humble confession, and happy restoration.

It was while Peter "tarried many days" that God opened for him new doors of ministry. Too often we push and shove, trying to open doors ourselves, only to have them slam shut on our fingers. From a human point of view, our Lord's ministry on earth was a dismal failure; but the Father knew what the Son had accomplished. It doesn't really matter that we are not rated with the top ten, so long as we do the Father's will and glorify him.

This is no excuse for laziness or mediocrity. Believers who know how to tarry will always do their best. And while they are doing it, they will experience a poise and adequacy that can come only from God.

Who knows? If all of us slowed down a bit, if we cancelled a few meetings from the church calendar, if we took time to wait before God in prayer, we might see God work in wonderful ways. We might see some fractured marriages mended again, some discordant ministries brought back into God's harmony, some exhausted believers given new strength and zeal for God. We might even see revival!

"Be still, and know that I am God" (Ps. 46:10).

26 WEIGHING THE CONVERTS

"Converts should be weighed as well as counted." Evangelist D. L. Moody made that statement, and his warning needs to be heeded today. Evangelical ministries seem to be mired in the Book of Numbers, convinced that exciting statistics are always the equivalent of spiritual realities. Sad to say, they are not.

Please do not conclude that I oppose growth. I am not among those exclusive saints who believe we should work harder and harder to reach fewer and fewer. Where there is spiritual life, there must be growth. If God's servants are faithfully sowing the seed, God must keep his promise and ultimately give the increase.

But I am afraid of the artificial kind of growth that is manufactured and sometimes exaggerated, growth that is not the true work of the Spirit of God. Our techniques are so refined these days that it is difficult to tell the difference. I am also afraid of the kind of human measurements that convince us that the structure is sound when it is actually about to topple and fall. We boast that we are "rich . . . and have need of nothing," when all the while we are "wretched, miserable, poor, blind, and naked" (Rev. 3:17). Instead of weeping over the X-ray photographs that tell the truth, we are reveling in the carefully retouched pictures that make everything look healthy.

Certainly we want to reach people! I often told the congregations that I pastored that we wanted crowds, not so that we could count people, but because people count. Our challenge is to reach a lost world with the gospel and not to build an elite mutual admiration society. "Fruit . . . more fruit . . . much fruit . . ." is still our Lord's desire, and this demands growth.

I am convinced that God's work grows more by nutrition than by addition. Paul described this growth in Colossians 2:19: "From which all the body by joints and bands having nourishment ministered, and knit together, increaseth with the increase of God." Spiritual growth, like physical growth, is from the inside out, and each part must make its own special contribution.

Too often, the growth in a local church is the byproduct of a one-man ministry (usually a dynamic leader) supported by a loyal staff and the approval of the church officers. There may be little nutrition from the Word of God, but there is a great deal of promotion. The members of the body are spectators, not participants. They not only do not use their spiritual gifts, but often do not even know what gifts they possess.

Imagine a mother who is told by the doctor that her baby is underweight. Instead of accurately diagnosing the cause and changing the diet, she visits the butcher and purchases several pounds of meat. This meat she somehow attaches to her baby's body. The baby is put on the scale—and lo!— the child is no longer underweight. However, the baby is now in worse condition than before. The mother has manufactured a temporary solution that blinds her to the real needs of her child. She has solved her problem by statistics, but she has not gotten to the root of the matter. Who has ears to hear, let them hear.

It is not easy to measure spiritual ministry, and God's servants need wisdom and discernment lest they think themselves poor when they are really rich (see Rev. 2:9). Paul ridiculed the statistical saints of his day when he wrote: "For we dare not class ourselves or compare ourselves with those who commend themselves. But they, measuring themselves by themselves, and comparing themselves among themselves, are not wise" (2 Cor. 10:12). We will never really know what was accomplished until we stand before our Lord and the holy fire tests our works. In that day, some who are last will be first; and some who think themselves first may end up at the back of the line.

I am fully aware of the fact that the Holy Spirit records numbers in the Book of the Acts: three thousand souls (2:41), then five thousand (4:4), and then "multitudes of both men and women" (5:14). But the Holy Spirit also recorded the conversion of one man—Saul of Tarsus. And behind the thousands of converts in the early days of the church is the conversion of Simon Peter who was brought to Jesus by Andrew, his brother (John 1:40–42). If converts are to be weighed, I wonder how much Paul and Peter tip the scales.

At all costs, we must avoid extremes. Spurgeon used to say that the people who criticized statistics usually had none to report. Too often, this is true. We must avoid wanting numbers simply for the sake of statistics, but we must also shun that complacent attitude that has as its motto, "Small is spiritual." The secret, I think, is to be concerned with individuals and to let God take care of the numbers. Jesus had time for individuals; they, in turn, helped him to reach the crowds. The woman of Samaria is a case in point (John 4).

If growth is from within—the "increase of God"—then it will glorify God and it will last. If growth is the result of nutrition, not manufactured addition, then it will strengthen God's church and bring honor to God's name. Moody was right: "Converts should be weighed as well as counted." And while we are weighing them, let's be careful to keep our thumbs off the scales!

27 Take Your Stand—The Right Way

There was a time when most evangelical Christians were satisfied with silence. When great issues were being discussed, the dedicated Christian watched and prayed and stayed out of the battle. For believers to be involved in politics or social issues meant that they had forsaken true Bible separation.

But now that day is over. Today, dedicated believers feel guilty if they fail to register their convictions about great moral and social issues. With the dawning of this new day, some new problems have emerged. If we do not solve these problems, our speaking out on issues will create more difficulties than did our guilty silence.

Perhaps the first problem involves *information*. Most of us are not experts in these fields. What we know about Bible translations, abortion, capital punishment, social welfare, and a host of other issues has been gathered secondhand. Our information is selective because most believers read only the literature that they agree with. This means that we have studied only one side of the issue, if we have studied even that. I am amazed at how many Christians consider themselves experts on complex issues simply because they have read a pamphlet or a magazine article.

This leads to the second problem—*the danger of manipulation*. A few writers and speakers can control the thinking of millions of people because their readers or listeners do not know any better. The word for this is *propaganda*. By using the techniques of propaganda (name-calling, half-truths, glittering generalities, and so on), clever writers or preachers can convince an audience that theirs is the only righteous cause. It is even possible to twist Scripture to defend their position.

Our third problem is *making these issues tests of spirituality and fellowship*. The enemy is out to divide God's people, and he finds plenty of ammunition available wherever believers disagree about matters that have high emotional content. At a time in history when the church desperately needs to be united in its witness, sad to say, we are divided on marginal issues. Instead of devoting our time and money spreading the gospel, we are busy in other activities that neither strengthen the saints nor win the lost.

There is a fourth problem—*speaking up on these issues in an immature manner*. I have read some of the letters sent by evangelical Christians to people in places of leadership, and I have been embarrassed. To be sure, not all letters are embarrassing, because there are still Christians who know how to disagree with others without being disagreeable. But some of our public servants must have a biased opinion of evangelical Christians after reading their mail.

Having said all of this, I am not suggesting that the church retreat into silent obscurity and never raise its voice in either approval or protest. But I do have some suggestions to make that might, if followed, sharpen our witness to an unbelieving world. The next time you plan to write a letter to anyone in a place of leadership, keep these suggestions in mind.

Get the facts straight. In other words, don't believe everything you hear or read. Be especially careful about signing petitions in the vestibule of the church. If you have ever played the party game "Gossip," then you know how "facts" can get garbled as they are "communicated" from one person to another. In recent years, the Federal Communications Commission was deluged with letters and petitions protesting a law that was not even being considered!

Beware of propaganda. Even well-meaning evangelicals can use name-calling or exaggeration in their zeal to defend truth and oppose lies. Never allow somebody to manipulate your thinking just to support a crusade. Take time to pray and to consider the issues calmly and with the facts before you.

Speak the truth in love. If you feel you ought to register your convictions, then do it in such a way that your letter will make it easier, not harder, for the next Christian to witness to the recipient. Many people in public offices are convinced that evangelical Christians are "cranks." (Some of the mail I have read has almost convinced me at times!) Practice the Golden Rule and write the kind of a letter you would want to receive yourself.

Don't get detoured. As the salt of the earth and the light of the world, we must make the principles of righteousness felt in our society. But our main task is not to protest corruption but to preach Christ. The heart of every problem is still the problem in the heart; and that problem can be solved only by the gospel. To devote your energy and time to some personal crusade while ignoring the Great Commission is to play right into the hands of the enemy.

I sometimes feel that the church today is like an adolescent who is trying out his newfound freedom of expression. In recent years, it has been popular to be a Christian, even a conservative born-again Christian. That popularity will not last forever, for the enemies of truth and righteousness will not stand by and do nothing. However, the time has come for us to mature and move out of that adolescent stage. Yes, we must make our convictions known; but let's be sure they are true convictions and not just shallow opinions or secondhand prejudices. Let's also be sure that we know what we are talking about, lest we embarrass the gospel by our zeal without knowledge.

Proverbs 18:13 might be a good text for all of us: "He who answers a matter before he hears it, it is folly and shame to him."

28 Dig Up Those Bitter Roots

hat one thing causes the most problems in a local church?" A young pastor asked me that question at a pastors' conference, and my reply (which drew several loud amens from others) was, "The thing Hebrews 12:15 warns about—a root of bitterness."

Here is what the passage says: "Pursue peace with all men, and holiness, without which no one shall see the Lord: looking diligently lest anyone fall short of the grace of God; lest any root of bitterness springing up cause trouble, and by this many become defiled" (Heb. 12:14–15).

By using the image of a root, the writer taught us a number of practical truths about bitterness in the human heart. For one thing, a root has to be planted. How does bitterness get planted in the heart? Usually it's by our getting hurt by something somebody has said or done and then holding a grudge against that person. It could happen in a church committee meeting or in private conversation. The culprit probably doesn't even know that he or she has hurt us. Instead of facing the matter openly and honestly, we bury it in our hearts; and a root of bitterness starts to grow.

But roots will not grow unless they are cultivated. If you and I would honestly confess our hurt and our sin to the Lord, he would help us pull up the root. This would save us a great deal of pain. The trouble is, we enjoy feeding our egos and cultivating the bitterness down inside. Outwardly, we maintain pious behavior, but inwardly, we are full of bitter poison.

Hidden sins do not stay hidden very long. A day and an hour comes when that root of bitterness springs up in bitter words or actions, and then everybody discovers what only God had known. Poison that has been brewing in the heart for weeks, perhaps years, suddenly erupts and infects everybody around us.

A root of bitterness causes trouble and defilement, according to the Scriptures. It never makes the bitter person better, nor does it improve the people in the home or the church. In fact, the root of bitterness troubles and defiles long before it is recognized openly. It is impossible for bitter believers not to have that hidden bitterness affect their praying, witnessing, fellowshiping, and serving. Because they are troubled and defiled, they trouble and defile everything around them; yet all the while, everything looks spiritual.

A root of bitterness must be dealt with drastically. It must be exposed and pulled up. The ax must be laid to the root of the tree. It does no good to break off the sick branches or pluck off the dead leaves; the trouble is at the roots. If you have ever had to dig up a tree root that was causing problems, then you know what a difficult task it is. This kind of spiritual surgery is never easy, but it is necessary.

Of course, the best approach is to keep the root from getting started in the first place. This takes effort, which explains why the writer used exhortations such as "follow peace" and "looking diligently" (vv. 14, 15). Just as the gardener must hate weeds and pull them up, so the believer must hate roots of bitterness and pull them up. And keep this in mind: It is easier to pull them up when they are small. The longer we wait, the deeper they grow and the more bitter the poison gets.

Three words tell us how to keep roots of bitterness out of the soil of the heart: "peace," "holiness," and "grace." If we are following peace with all men, we will obey our Lord's instructions in Matthew 18:15–20, and we will not permit hurt feelings to break our fellowship with our brothers and sisters. If we are cultivating holiness of life, the atmosphere will simply not permit roots of bitterness to thrive. All of this we do by the grace of God. By nature, we want to defend ourselves and get what is coming to us (and perhaps give others what we think is coming to them). But the grace of God changes all of that.

It is foolish to waste time and energy cultivating roots of bitterness when we could be cultivating the fruit of the Spirit. It is next to impossible for bitter roots to grow successfully where love, joy, and peace are flourishing. Bitterness would be crowded out! And the harvest of the Spirit is much more beautiful and enjoyable than an ugly root of bitterness.

The grace of God never fails, but we might fail to appropriate the grace of God if we refuse to heed this warning. Perhaps the time has come for some of us to examine the soil of our hearts.

29 ONE WORLD AT A TIME

*W*hen American naturalist Henry David Thoreau lay dying, his friend Parker Pillsbury visited him and, in the course of a strained conversation, said, "You seem so near the brink of the dark river, that I almost wonder how the opposite shore may appear to you."

Thoreau quietly replied, "One world at a time."

That witty reply has often been quoted with approval, but I wonder if the people who approve it really know what they are doing. While Thoreau was a good man, he was not a confessed Christian. When an old friend of the family asked him about his relationship to Christ, Thoreau replied that "a snowstorm was more to him than Christ."

"One world at a time" is really an excellent philosophy of life *if you choose the right world*. If you live for this world, then you will lose the world to come. But if you choose the world to come, you will have both it and the blessings that God puts into this world for our good and his glory.

This is the message Jesus tried to get across in that penetrating address we call the Sermon on the Mount. "But seek ye first the kingdom of God, and his righteousness," he promised, "and all these things shall be added unto you" (Matt. 6:33).

A Christian attempts the impossible when he tries to live in two worlds at the same time. There is no such thing as sacred and secular in the Christian life, because everything comes from God and belongs to God. Paul admonishes us to "trust . . . in the living God, who gives us richly all things to enjoy" (1 Tim. 6:17). The best way to enjoy the world that God has made is to let your life be motivated and controlled by the world to come.

After all, believers are strangers and pilgrims in this world. Everything in believers' lives should belong to heaven. Their citizenship is in heaven, their home is in heaven, and their Savior is in heaven. We want our treasures to be in heaven, and they will be if we are living for the world to come.

Let's think of the benefits that we gain when we put God first and live one world at a time, the world of the will of God.

First, this kind of dedication *unifies our lives*. Compromising Christians live a divided life. They are trying to look in two directions, love two masters, live for two rewards; and that kind of life always self-destructs.

There is something dynamic and compelling about a life that is unified. "This one thing I do!" wrote Paul, and we today benefit from Paul's dedication. "For to me, to live is Christ!" When you build your life around the will and the purpose of God, you keep your life from falling apart. Consecration leads to concentration, and concentration leads to power.

There is a second benefit that we enjoy when we live one world at a time: *We simplify our lives*. Remember the last time you had to pack your belongings and move? If you said it once, you said it perhaps a dozen times: "How did I accumulate all this junk?" Most of us go through life carrying far more baggage than God ever required, and we wonder why life gets complicated.

While I do not agree with Thoreau's religious beliefs, I must confess that he had some good things to say about this matter of simplifying our lives. He once said that a man's wealth is measured by the amount of things he can afford to do without. As he watched the busy people of Concord from his window, he wrote: "Only that traveling is good which reveals to me the value of home and enables me to enjoy it better." I wonder what he would write if he could see the rushing passengers at O'Hare or the traffic in New York City!

I believe that the Scriptures encourage a life of simplicity. Jesus warned that our lives are not measured by the amount of things we accumulate or by the number of activities we are involved in (see Luke 12:15). Jesus became poor to make us rich, but we have determined to become rich, and thus we make ourselves poor.

All of us are grateful for the comforts of life, but we need to beware lest these creature comforts become masters instead of servants. It is good to have the things that money can buy provided we don't lose the things that money can't buy. There is a vast difference between prices and values, and some people are paying too high a price for the small returns they get on their investment.

When you live one world at a time and when that world is the world to come, it unifies and simplifies your life. But it also dignifies your life. It lifts you above the madding crowd and its foolish striving after wind. In his Sermon on the Mount, Jesus shamed his listeners (and us today) by pointing out that nothing in all of nature worries except man. The birds trust their Father to feed them, and the lilies know that God will adorn them with beauty. But man continues to worry! "What shall we eat? What shall we drink? What shall we put on?" (see Matt. 6:25–34).

We are made in the image of God, yet too often we live lower than the animals.

This leads us to a fourth benefit that comes when we put Christ first and live "one world at a time": *It glorifies God.* "Therefore, whether you eat or drink, or whatever you do, do all to the glory of God" (1 Cor. 10:31). I wonder if it glorifies God for parents to be so busy in church work that they neglect their own children. Or for pastors to be so occupied with seminars and denominational gatherings that they ignore the needs and opportunities in their own churches.

I can recall a time in my ministry when I thought it glorified God to have a full schedule, with many meetings in many places; but I have long since changed my mind. I realize that there are some people (like the apostle Paul) whom God has called to minister in many places and have no settled home. But I think that he has called most of us to glorify him by centering in on the one task he has given us and to do that task the very best we can.

In recent years I have learned to use the word *no*. I have been misunderstood and criticized—one of my friends is convinced that I'm backslidden!—but I feel I'm doing what God wants me to do. I'm trying to practice Matthew 6:33, and it isn't easy. There are many thrilling opportunities for service these days, and I wish I could be a part of all of them. But if I were involved in all of them, I would do none of them really well; and the result would be a broken body and a limited ministry.

Many church members have the mistaken notion that the "celebrity Christians" will get the greatest reward in heaven, but I have my doubts about that evaluation. I have a feeling that it will be the unknown faithful saints in local churches and in Christian homes who will receive our Lord's highest praise. It will be the faithful pastors and Sunday-school teachers who stayed by the stuff and did

the work God called them to do. It will be the dedicated mothers and fathers who raised godly children and sent them off to serve the Lord.

In one of the churches I pastored, there was a retired schoolteacher who ministered in the primary department of our Sunday school. She was a tiny lady who was not given to promoting herself, but what a prayer warrior she was! She kept a list of the names of all the pupils who went through her class, and she prayed for them faithfully until they were converted. Often she came to me after a baptismal service and said, "Pastor, I've been praying for years for several of the people you baptized tonight. They used to be in my class."

That dear Christian lady lived one world at a time, and it was the right world! To the best of my knowledge, she has never spoken at a women's retreat or taught a seminar, nor has she ever been interviewed for Christian radio or the press; but she is one of God's great saints, and she will be rewarded. When I was her pastor, people gave me credit for what was happening in the church; but the Lord knew, and I knew, that the blessings came because of people like her who were living in kingdom come.

It isn't easy to live one world at a time. It means you must have the courage to decide to put Christ first and the strength to hold to that decision; but the Lord's grace makes this possible. "By the grace of God, I am what I am," wrote Paul; and we must follow his example.

When you live one world at a time, you look at life from God's point of view. You ask yourself, "What will this be worth one hundred years from now—or in eternity?"

Perhaps the time has come for us to dismantle the ancient scaffolding that clutters our lives, homes, and churches. Like Martha, we are anxious and distracted by many things, "but one thing is needful." Like Mary, we must choose "that good part" which can never be taken from us.

It's time for us to start living one world at a time and making sure it is God's world—his kingdom and his righteousness—that controls our values and our goals.

It's time to start living with eternity's values in view.

30 BACK TO THE FATHER AND HOME

The opposite of being content is being troubled. Jesus said in John 14:1, "Let not your heart be troubled." We have discovered that God's answer for troubled nations, troubled churches, and troubled believers is found in John 14:6: "I am the way, the truth, and the life. No one comes to the Father except through Me." It is also God's answer for troubled sinners—those who do not know Jesus Christ as their Savior.

If you are not a believer in Jesus Christ, you ought to be troubled—troubled about your destiny and about the fact that you are missing so much that God has for you in this life. You ought also to be troubled about your future apart from God. So, if you do not know Jesus Christ as your Savior, I want you to pay close attention to John 14:6.

This verse is illustrated in Luke 15. Jesus told a parable about a father and his two boys—an older brother and a younger brother. In this parable of the prodigal son, (the word *prodigal* means "wasteful"), the younger brother wasted his substance in riotous living.

As you read this account, notice the condition of this boy: he was lost (see v. 24); he was also ignorant—verse 17 says, "when he came to himself;" and he was dead—"For this my son was dead" (v. 24). These are the characteristics of all unsaved people: lost, ignorant, and spiritually dead.

People like to measure themselves by themselves. Many lost people argue, "I'm as good as the people at the church! In fact, I'm probably better!" But God does not measure one sinner against another sinner. God measures us by his own standard of holiness. When you and I can say that we are like Jesus Christ, then God will accept us.

So let's stop comparing ourselves with each other, and admit that every unsaved person is like this boy. First, he was *lost*. What does it mean to be lost? It means to be in a place of danger. It means to be at a distance from the God whom we ought to love and serve.

In Luke 15, there are actually three parables: the lost sheep, the lost coin, and the lost son. The lost sheep was in a place of danger and could not find his way home. The lost coin was useless. You can't spend a coin that is lost! And the lost son was away from the joy and the fellowship that he could have had at home. If you have never received Jesus Christ, you are lost—not geographically, but spiritually. You are in the far country. You ask, "How far away is that far country?" It's just one step away from God, one step outside of God's will.

Second, this young man was *ignorant*. Luke 15:17 says, "when he came to himself." Up to that point, this fellow had been beside himself, blinded by sin, blinded by the world and the flesh. He thought that he could find joy and satisfaction out there in the world—out in the far country—but everything he lived on ran out. The circumstances around him became unbearable. Anybody looking at him would have said, "You know, that boy is really stupid. At home he has protection and provision, he has fellowship and love; yet here he is starving alone in this far country. The pigs are better off than he is, because they have someone to take care of them; but no one is taking care of him."

Third, he was *dead.* Of course, he wasn't physically dead; otherwise he wouldn't be able to arise and go to his father. He was *spiritually* dead. He was away from his father's life, love, and blessings. If you do not know Jesus as your Savior, this is your condition. You may be moral, you may be religious, and you may be the kindest of neighbors; but if you have never trusted Christ, you are *lost*—you are away from the Father's home; you are *ignorant*—you are away from the Father's blessing and truth; and you are *dead*—you are away from the Father's life.

What did the prodigal son have to do to change all of this? He had to make a decision. He said, "I will arise." Salvation involves the whole person—the mind, the emotions, and the will. With his mind he said, "How many hired servants of my father's have bread enough and to spare?" (v. 17). With his emotions he said, "I perish with hunger" (v. 17). And with his will he said, "I will arise" (v. 18). Salvation involves all three. You can know the truth, and you can feel the need for Jesus; but until you say, "I will arise and go to my Father!" God cannot save you.

There are two aspects to our salvation—the human and the divine. Salvation is wholly of grace, but it is not forced upon a person. The lost sheep didn't find its way home—the shepherd went out looking for the sheep. The lost coin didn't come rolling out—the woman looked for the coin. Salvation begins with God's love for the lost sinner. But in this third parable of Luke 15 that *the father did not go out to look for the son.* The father waited for the son to say, "I will." There are two aspects to salvation. There is God's part—God seeks the lost sinner. "The Son of Man has come to seek and to save that which was lost," reads Luke 19:10. This is God's work of grace. But there is also a personal response to that grace. "I will arise and go!"

We don't fully understand all of this. This is one of the mysteries that we don't fathom yet; but we know it is true.

Jesus Christ appeals to the will when he says, "Come." This boy said, "I will arise and go to my father." The only other place I know of in the New Testament that talks about going to the Father is John 14:6. Let's put this verse beside Luke 15 and see the parallel. This boy was *lost*, and Jesus said, "I am the way." The boy was *ignorant*, and Jesus said, "I am the truth." This boy was *dead*, and Jesus said, "I am the life."

How do you come to the Father? Through Jesus Christ! You may be saying, "Yes, I agree with that—I am lost, I'm wandering, I'm in the far country. I've run out of satisfaction and sustenance, and I'm ready to quit. Do you mean that Jesus Christ is the way to the Father? "Yes, he is, the *only* way.

You may say, "Well, I've been ignorant. I thought I could live in sin and get away with it. I thought I could get out here in the world and I'd enjoy life; but I realize that true satisfaction is not in sin. I've been stupid!" But Jesus says, "I am the truth." We will take you to the Father.

And if you say, "Yes, I'm dead in sin, I realize this—I'm lost, I'm ignorant, and I'm dead," Jesus answers, "I am the life"; he will take you to the Father.

For Jesus Christ to be the Way, the Truth, and the Life, to take us to the Father, he had to suffer and die on the cross. It is interesting to note that in the Gospel of John, Jesus used the phrase *lifted up* three times. Now, by "lifted up" he doesn't mean exalted; he doesn't mean being put high on a pedestal. By "lifted up" he means crucified. In John 12:32, Jesus said, "And I, if I am lifted up from the earth [crucifixion], will draw all peoples to Myself." Not everyone without exception, but everyone without distinction—Jews and Gentiles, rich and poor, wise and unwise. He had to be lifted up to draw people to God. He is the way. He had to die that he might open this true and living way.

"Then said Jesus to them, 'When you lift up the Son of Man, then you will know that I am He" (John 8:28). He was lifted up that he might draw people in *the way,* and he was lifted up that he might reveal to people *the truth.* "As Moses lifted up the serpent in the wilderness, even so must the Son of Man be lifted up, that whoever believes in Him should not perish but have eternal life." He was lifted up that people might have the way, know the truth, and receive the life.

Are you troubled today by your sin? I hope you are! I hope you realize how foolish a thing it is to live in sin. If you are troubled by your sin and by the thought of some-day facing God, listen to Jesus' words in John 14:6. If you want to come to the Father, simply open your heart to Jesus Christ; for he is the only One who can save you and take you to the Father.

Jesus Christ is the Way, the Truth, and the Life. He is God's final and perfect remedy for troubled nations, troubled churches, troubled hearts, and troubled sinners. "Let not your heart be troubled."